# Poppies and Snowdrops

# Poppies and Snowdrops

*Resources for Times of*
*Grief and Bereavement*

Andrew Pratt and
Marjorie Dobson

# Poppies and Snowdrops

## Resources for Times of Grief and Bereavement

Andrew Pratt and
Marjorie Dobson

Copyright © Andrew Pratt and Marjorie Dobson
Cover image of snowdrops © Patricia Ronald, other images © LiquidLibrary

British Library Cataloguing in Publication data
A catalogue record for this book is available
from the British Library

ISBN 1-85852-308-7
ISBN 978-1-85852-308-8

First published by Inspire
4 John Wesley Road
Werrington
Peterborough PE4 6ZP

Printed and bound in Great Britain by
Stanley L Hunt (Printers) Ltd
Rushden, Northants

# Foreword

Grief is a lonely business. It leaves us shocked, desolate, disabled and sometimes disbelieving – but most of all, it is heartbreakingly lonely. Just as our love and relationship with the one we've lost is unique, so too is the grieving that follows. There are no time limits, no short cuts, no pills, rules or comparisons worth making. It hurts, it haunts – and everyone's grief is their own.

And because each path of grief is individual, one bereaved person's needs can be sharply at odds with the needs of another. How often have we seen couples, who have been lovingly united for years, growing apart following the loss of someone they both love? One partner might feel the need to talk their feelings through with those around them, questioning, raging, reasoning, perhaps even fighting for justice. Through sharing and talking endlessly about their love and loss, they hope to find their way to understanding, accepting and moving on with their grief. Their partner, on the other hand, might only seek solace within themselves, holding the pain and questions inside, not able to articulate or share their feelings even with those dearest to them. How could anyone else possibly begin to understand what they alone are going through? And so they push loving friends away, shunning outstretched arms – and that must surely be the loneliest grief of all.

So often grief is accompanied by fear – fear of a very different life ahead. Can you possibly be happy again? How will you cope alone, not just emotionally but in so many practical ways too? How will you be in a crowd on your own, no longer part of a couple but 'single' in every sense of the word? How long before you can listen to the radio without lines from familiar songs searing into your heart? Or smell that perfume? Glimpse that photo? Think you hear the voice you long for, knowing it can't be so?

I remember so well a time of great loss and confusion in my own life, when it felt as if the bottom had dropped out of the world I knew, and I was falling helplessly out of control. I've prayed all my life – but at that time, it felt as if my prayers were heard by no one. It wasn't that I believed God was not there. I never doubted his existence for one moment. I simply couldn't feel him. It was as if he was keeping his distance, watching from afar as I stumbled. The presence that had been my dearest friend for a lifetime seemed to desert me when I needed him most.

It was at my lowest point that someone very wise said to me, 'When your heart is broken, God takes care of all the little pieces.' That didn't make sense at the time – not until I made the decision to stop being *re*-active to everything that came my way, and start being *pro*-active, getting on with the process of reshaping my life with all the gifts and opportunities available to me.

That was the turning point. I made a choice, and suddenly understood that God, having allowed me the freedom of choice, was there in a very real sense to support me through. I became aware of his love through others – the neighbours who turned up at the door with casseroles and toolboxes for our new home; the old friends who didn't mind my 3 a.m. phone calls, responding with a shoulder to cry on and a listening ear.

Slowly, so slowly, with their and God's help, I began the journey upwards, stronger, wiser and more aware than ever of God's loving presence when we need him most. Through such challenges, we become what he knows we can be. He *does* take care of all the little pieces – fixed back together, perhaps never quite the same again, but all the stronger for it.

How I wish, though, that I'd had this book through that desolate, confusing time! It's full of wisdom, compassion, understanding and inspiration. Within its covers you'll find so much to support you wherever you are on life's path. Sometimes it's just a small phrase that speaks to you alone, a few words of encouragement that touch the rawest of your nerves with soothing comfort. On your journey of grief, this book could be your cherished companion.

Pam Rhodes

# Acknowledgements

First of all we would like to thank Natalie Watson and the staff of *mph* who have been unfailingly kind and helpful towards us as we have prepared this collection.

We would like to acknowledge the help of June Baker and David McCarthy in generously providing tunes for this book and Damian Boddy for his guidance with music.

Stainer & Bell Ltd and CJM Music Ltd have been helpful in providing copyright material for inclusion.

We are grateful to all those who have shared stories or offered comments to us, as we have used this material with them or offered it to them for reflection.

Ron and Jackie, our spouses, have put up with us and coped with our absences while we have worked to put this collection together. We thank them.

Last, but not least, we thank our families without whom this book would not have been written.

# Contents

# Poppies and snowdrops

A blood red symbol of the field of war,
the poppy stands and bows its head before
the wind that sweeps its petals to the skies,
until the field is black and colour dies.

A frail, white symbol of a winter passed,
the snowdrop's bud breaks through iron ground at last
and, with bravado, lifts a fragile flower,
defiant through each icy, wintry shower.

A memory, a hope, one red, one white:
red comforts and white sings through sorrow's night.

# Introduction

This collection tries to offer resources for individuals, for those who are bereaved and for those who try to care for them. All the material has come out of real situations and is offered to those who live with the reality of death.

Here are hymns that offer the possibility of singing what it would be difficult to say. Poems, meditations and prayers offer the opportunity to express thoughts that are otherwise suppressed. Dramatic readings may be imaginative internal monologue, yet express common human emotions. Blessings are included, some for the ending of worship, but most to be used as a personal benediction, echoing the Celtic tradition which is of words to carry away for meditation.

A funeral liturgy is included for use in situations where most of the congregation have no experience of the Christian faith. There is material for use on inter-faith occasions; pieces that could be used at times of remembrance and many items for personal reflection. These include an 'almost lullaby' that could be used by a carer and sung to a 'home-made' tune.

It is our belief that everyone is valued by God. This value should be recognized in this life, through death and beyond. It is not limited by time, in the human sense. So the book begins with a reminder of the value of each individual to God. Each person is a unique and valued child of God. Eternal life starts here. This is a statement backed up by the Bible and the thread of this understanding is woven through the collection.

We explore our own experience as human beings and that of people with whom we have shared in a variety of ways. Life is limited and for some the limitations come through disabling illness, which is sometimes terminal. This affects not only those who are watching and caring, but also the person who is living with the disability, who is dying.

Death is sometimes sudden with no time to prepare, no time to say 'goodbye'. Suicide brings questions, doubts and recriminations. Children should outlive their parents. That is not always the case. Natural disasters, terrorism or genocide can affect a whole nation, fuelling anxiety.

However death occurs, those who grieve have feelings. Doubt and denial can mix with anger and depression and somehow each person has to cope with the loss and the emotions she has as a consequence. We do our best to care for one another. Time is taken to listen. We do necessary practical things. A funeral is arranged if there is a body. Services of thanksgiving take place. Ritual provides comfort or rides roughshod over the bereaved.

Beyond all this faith comes or is lost, or grows again in a new beginning, in which we learn to live with the fact of the death of the one we have loved. Sometimes old feelings surge back again and cover us like waves.

Yet it is our belief that somehow love, God's love, remains. For 'there is nothing in all creation' ... not even death ... 'that can separate us from the love of God'. It is our hope that that statement of faith may one day become a reality for all who share this book.

We understand that feelings of grief can be associated with losses other than death – redundancy, divorce, or separation, and many other experiences – but it is beyond the scope of this collection to address these.

Scripture passages are taken from the New Revised Standard Version or from translations produced by the authors of this collection.

Marjorie Dobson and Andrew Pratt

# All God's children

*Each one of us matters to God however we see ourselves, however low or depressed we may feel. As the Psalmist prayed, 'Guard me as the apple of the eye; hide me in the shadow of your wings' (Psalm 17.8). And God responds, 'Do not fear, for I have redeemed you; I have called you by name, you are mine' (Isaiah 43.1).*

# A child of God

A child of God
thrust into the world
wrinkled, red-faced and bloodied,
yelling for breath.
Unaware
of the indignity of birth;
needing food, sleep, protection.
Vulnerable,
yet brimming with possibilities.

A child of God,
rebellious youth.
Argumentative, opinionated;
constantly searching;
experimenting dangerously;
unaware
of the consequences.
Hurtling headlong
into the future.

A child of God
searching for love.
Looking for perfection
through complex emotions
of compromise.
Totally aware
of vulnerability;
yet restless in the quest
for fulfillment.

A child of God,
mature adult;
stressed, burdened and troubled
by responsibilities.
Barely aware
of mortality.
Only concerned to appear
successful.
Coping with life.

A child of God
preparing to die.
Wrinkled and pale,
struggling for breath.
Aware
of the indignity
of helplessness.
Waiting for sleep.
Looking to new life.
Completion!

# Through faith I feel that in your sight

Through faith I feel that in your sight
I have intrinsic worth,
for you have watched my every step
and loved me from my birth.

My falt'ring steps, my childish play,
discovery, delight:
at every stage you helped me grow,
you kept me in your sight.

And now as others point and stare,
devalue and despise,
O God, I need to know your love
and see it in your eyes.

So look on me and show that love
that once had seemed so sure,
and through the care of faithful friends
be there to reassure.

Tune:  Fingal (Anderson)
Metre:  CM

# Friend! sing above your circumstance

Friend! sing above your circumstance,
for that is how you're seen
by God who holds you in such love,
knows what you should have been.

Catastrophe has scarred your life,
your lot has pushed you down:
a helter-skelter ride of fate,
yet grace is still your ground.

A partner of the precedent
that cannot be destroyed:
with Christ an heir to holy love,
faith's end you can't avoid.

So, in that strength, raise up your head,
hold out against the foe,
defeat this dying with God's love
and let God's spirit blow.

Tune:  Attercliffe (Mather)
Metre:  CM

*Even in bleak times God is with us though we cannot always recognize that. In fact to state this is sometimes the most insensitive thing to do. We need to hear one another and to respond to what we hear, not what we wish we'd heard. Nevertheless we can affirm what we feel to be true and sometimes, often much later, even years later, that truth may be grasped.*

# One single word

One single word
spoken at the right time
can make all the difference.

This is a good time.
Today I'm cloud-walking,
clear skies above,
head and shoulders above everything else,
treading on air
with cotton wool beneath my feet.

Life is good.

For once, I feel achievement
bolstering my confidence.
There is praise and respect
and people look at me
in a different light.

But it won't last ...

Lord, keep me safe
when suddenly the clouds fall away,
when turbulence is inevitable,
when I must come down
from dizzy heights
and touch the earth again.

Grant me a safe landing
and the ability to keep going
and to maintain my faith
until it is time to take off again.

# Are you there, God?

Are you there, God?
Because, if you're not, I'm ready to give up altogether.
Nobody else seems to care about me.
They tell me I'm useless. Not worth bothering about.
I feel totally insignificant. So unloved.
I've never had any support. No encouragement.
People give up on me. Even my own family.
And I have no friends. No real friends.

What's the point of it all?
Is life always going to be as empty as this?
I need to hear someone talk to me as if they love me and value me.
Will you do that for me?
Please?
I seem to remember that Jesus called you 'father'.
Will you be my loving father, too?

# Some people look at me

Some people look at me as if I'm not human.
It wasn't my fault that I was born like this.
But when you're not the same, some people can't cope with that.
They bully, or call me names, or stare, or play on my weaknesses – know that I can't fight back.
Why are they so cruel?
Why is life so unfair?

God, do you love me?
Am I really made in your image, as the kind and loving ones try to tell me?
Are they telling the truth?

I really need to know!

*When things are going right it's sensible to praise. In this way we can build up a sort of account of faith to draw on when things are bad. Something like a third of all the Psalms are laments – complaints against God. That sort of complaint is possible, if we believe in God, and we trust that God believes in us and values us. Then when things go wrong, it's all right to complain.*

# The love of God is vast

The love of God is vast,
beyond imagination;
and worlds beyond the world we see
are held within creation.

The love of God brings hope,
to counter consternation;
a love that's perfect, casts out fear,
to kindle expectation.

The love of God forms faith,
and through participation
makes real the hope for which we long,
love's final consummation.

Tune:    The love of God is vast (June Baker)
Metre:   6.7.8.7.

# Tune: The love of God is vast

June Baker (1936- )

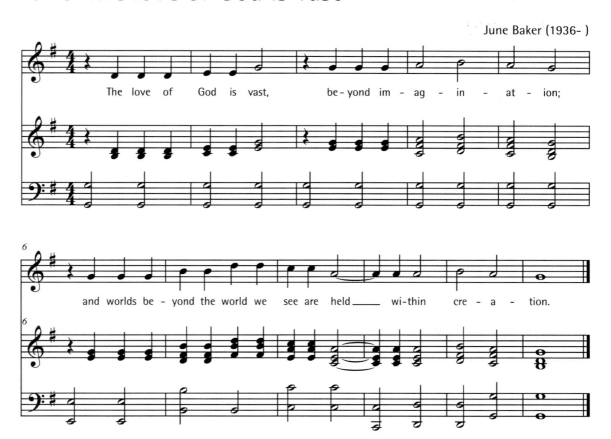

The love of God is vast, be-yond im - ag - in - at - ion;

and worlds be - yond the world we see are held ____ wi-thin cre - a - tion.

# How shall we praise the love of God

How shall we praise the love of God,
or celebrate its height?
Such love can never be confined,
nor we escape its sight.

God's love will always persevere,
it voices no tirade,
it is not proud, but always kind,
this love makes no parade.

God keeps no score of any wrong
and, like a burnished shield,
such love protects us from ourselves;
God's love will never yield.

There is no place that we can go,
no height to range above,
nor any depth that we can plumb,
outside this scale of love;

God's love is stronger than our fear,
it lasts beyond our breath,
it will not let us go in life,
will hold us after death.

Tune:    Belmont
Metre:   CM

Scriptures that might be helpful – Psalm 139;
1 Corinthians 13; Romans 8.28-39.

# Unknown, unknowing you have shown

Unknown, unknowing you have shown
enfolding warmth and care;
though clouds have hid you from our sight
your love was always there.

But like a hand we cannot see,
yet know, for sure, and feel,
you held, and never let us go:
we found your love was real.

And still, today, that love is firm,
though you are out of sight,
and nothing now, below, above,
can prise us from your might.

Tune:    Contemplation (Ouseley)
Metre:   CM

*No matter how strong our faith, how sure we are of God's love, we are not protected from pain and those around us die. Eventually we will die. Dying is part of being human. Knowing that does not make coping with death any easier. Just as surely as leaves change to gold in autumn, so lives change and weaken and people around us die.*

# These leaves will fall, decay and mould away

These leaves will fall, decay and mould away,
the garment of each life will wear and fray,
the fading colours tell that time has past,
but love and grace and hope and mem'ries last.

God gives a passing shadow that will fade
but never loses love for all that's made,
God treasures up for heaven each design,
each person is unique to the divine.

So live and love in knowing you are held
within this life, and on beyond as well.
Your God protects you going out and in,
this life on earth is just where you begin.

Tune:     Eventide
Metre:   10.10.10.10

*Through all the chances and changes of life, we remain valuable to God and we ought to remain valuable to each other. We are all unique and valued children of God.*

# Anxiety

O God, there are times when I am so afraid of the future,
because the older I get, the less there is of it.
I cover my fear by activity, by cheerfulness, by boasting of my age;
but deep within, I have a fear of the unknown
and I cannot hide that from you.
Compassionate God,
please look on my doubts and concerns with understanding.
Remind me of the number of times Jesus tells me not to be anxious.
Continue to show me purpose in my life
and assurance of your concern for me.
Talk to me of 'many rooms' and 'preparing a place' for me.
Then, loving God, surround me with the comforting warmth of your love,
so that my faith will be strengthened
and my hope renewed,
until I know the joy of coming home to you.

# Blessings

Through childhood and youth,
through maturity to age,
from life to death ...
to life again,
God will bless you and watch over you.

In the vulnerability and searching of youth;
in the troubles and cares of adulthood;
in the insecurity and anxiety of old age,
God holds us and cares for us as his children.
Thanks be to God.

# At life's limits

*terminal illness, dementia,
waiting for death*

*All people are valuable to God. But in the eyes of society the value of people can be limited. We can even feel of little value ourselves. My father, living with multiple sclerosis and lung cancer, asked 'what's the point of living?' Not just a question for him, but for those of us who cared as we tried to look after him and make life worthwhile. And he could understand.*
*Dementia, Alzheimer's disease raises profound questions for carers. And grief can begin long before a loved one dies. How can we cope? Where is God in all of this?*

# Echoes

Confused, alone, she sat,
not deep in the chair, but on the edge of it.
Her fingers twisting in an endless circle
of emptiness.
Eyes seeing nothing we could follow.
Mind in a distant place beyond our reach.
No flicker of recognition or welcome
from the one who had cradled me,
nurtured me, waited eagerly for my step
inside the door each day.

Words were no use, we thought.
This was a bad day
and she would never know we had been there
watching the disintegration
of her fiery, independent spirit;
the slow loss –
although today she was gone from us already.

Elsewhere rustles of interest
told the arrival of the keyboard player
with tattered books of music
from a bygone age
and those who could, gathered in
    chattering flock
to finger-tap and listen.

And then, among melodies familiar with age,
came 'bright and beautiful' and 'creatures
    great and small,'
and a thin, clear voice from that lonely chair
joined in a chorus from some childhood time.
Life gave its echo back to us
and brought the tears.

*Even those who do not recognize us are still the people we know. Perceptions may be distorted, names may be confused and the reality in which we live may no longer be shared, but this person is still known by God and still loved.*

# Lord, we ask your blessing on this confused mind

Lord, we ask your blessing on this confused mind.
You know that the experiences and knowledge of a lifetime are locked away
    inside a complicated mechanism to which this disease has inappropriate keys.

Keep this troubled one safe in confusion,
happy in forgetfulness,
aware in times of lucidity
and secure in the environment of constant care.

When there is fear and anger, surround her with your peace.
When despair strikes, give her your glimmer of hope.
When there seems to be no response, probe deep into the apparent emptiness of
    the mind with the reassurance of your love.

And when everything seems hopeless and this disease has full control, we
    commit her to your eternal compassion and care.

*Caring can be a long process. The following words are an expression of commitment, spoken from a carer to a loved one who is suffering; perhaps a daughter to her mother or a husband to a wife. Words to read or to sing as an 'almost lullaby'.*

# Here is your food and my arms to enfold you

Here is your food and my arms
    to enfold you,
love from the heart as you
    move toward death,
held out in hope that will comfort
    and hold you
through days of longing as
    life loses breath.

People you know are now hard to remember,
memories diminish, your body is frail;
things are left waiting you thought
    you would finish,
God will not leave you, and love will not fail.

I am beside you and God your companion,
will wait, will not leave you, will care
    and sustain.
Passing through life on to heaven's dominion,
faculties fade, but God's love will not wane.

*... and then a prayer.*

# Healing God

Healing God, reach out to the lives
of those who are sick in mind or body.
Medical science does not have the solutions
    to all problems,
so we pray especially for those people for
    whom no cure can be found.

Comfort and sustain them
as they cope with their problems
and give them your peace in their
    darkest times.
Help those who are with them –
relatives, friends, carers and medical staff –
to be strong in their support and
    compassionate in their care,
even though they too are under great stress.

Teach us to see life from their perspective
and to be alert to their particular needs.

*To care for someone with a terminal illness confronts us with so many different feelings. Often there remains a hope that through some immense miracle the person for whom we are caring will recover. At the other end of the scale is bleakness, as we come face to face with the reality that this is not going to happen and we begin to grieve for a loss that is not yet. Caring day after day, night after night, takes its toll. Life is finite and we don't want to 'take time off', yet we need respite and rest just to keep going. Roles are sometimes reversed with adult children caring in an intimate way for parents. Actions are repeated again and again. Frustration sets in and we feel angry. Then we feel guilty about feeling angry. At worst we feel helpless and hopeless.*

# When our caring love wears thin

When our caring love wears thin,
when our nerves are stretched and taut
and the strain of our concern
fills our every waking thought –
God of understanding heart,
give us strength to play our part.

When we watch in helpless love
when all hope of health is past
and distress cries out in pain
that this suffering will not last –
God of healing, hold us near,
bring your calm and drive out fear.

When our tears speak out our love,
when by smiles we mask our grief,
in those dark and lonely hours
when the silence mocks belief –
God of comfort, to our night
bring the dawning of your light.

\*When the one we loved has gone,
when death brings tormented peace,
as emotions swirl around –
sorrow mingled with release.
God of patience, bear our pain;
turn us back to life again.

*\*Last verse should be omitted when inappropriate*

Tune:   Lucerna Laudonie
Metre:  77.77.77

# Compassionate God

Compassionate God, you understand the burden of care that I carry.
You know that I do this as an act of love, but you also understand how difficult it is for me at times.
And I can be honest with you.
When I am at the end of my patience, grant me a breathing space.
When I want to shout and scream with frustration, open the safety valve that I need.
When I am so tired that I cannot think straight, grant me that essential spark of energy
    I need to keep me going.
When I cannot bear to watch the pain, keep that agony from showing in my eyes.
When I long for a merciful death for this one I love, hold me and grant me peace.
Dear God, help me to keep working and loving until this suffering is over.

*For the person who is dying the perspective is different. Jean-Dominique Bauby's book* The Diving-Bell and the Butterfly *was written after Bauby suffered a massive stroke. The following words were inspired by the book:*

# When limbs are just a source of pain

When limbs are just a source of pain,
and hope has ebbed away,
I dream of all that might have been,
I strain for God and pray.
Is death the freedom that I seek?
Are miracles just lies?
Or is a deeper wholeness found
beyond my human sighs?

My prayer? A talisman of dreams
of things that still might be;
I dare to taunt and plead again
for God to set me free.

A twisted sideshow for my friends,
a testing ground for faith:
I find myself an oddity,
a challenge to God's grace.
And so I wait within this room
for solitude to run,
for death to wake my dying eyes
to some bright morning sun.

# We pray for those who are struggling with pain

We pray for those who are struggling with pain and illness and who grow weary with the fight. We remember and ask for your blessing in their weakness. Families and friends are also involved in this struggle and face their own difficulties in watching the sufferings of those they love – as well as being a part of the caring and healing process. We pray especially for those who know that their battle with illness will not be won, for their burden is great.

*Confronting death, how do we cope? How do we even describe it?*

# This is the point of passing

This is the point of passing
when life returns through death,
when reason loses meaning,
existence seems unblessed.

This is the point of testing
when hope is frail as dust;
when faithfulness is languid
and fear destroys our trust.

This is the point of challenge:
to hold what we believe;
or open to the vastness
of all God can conceive.

This is the point for changing
to reassess our place,
to walk beyond the threshold,
to grasp God's boundless grace.

This is the point of dying,
perspective sharpened, honed;
God's love, we find, is endless,
while life we share is loaned.

*'Into your hands, O God, I commit my spirit' (Luke 23.36)*

*It was once thought right to record a dying person's last words. Some of these words are immensely inspiring. On his death bed John Wesley said 'Best of all is God is with us'. Even at the point of death, he sensed the nearness of the God he had served throughout his life.*

# Best of all is God is with us

Best of all is God is with us,
God will hold and never fail.
Keep that truth when storms are raging,
God remains though faith is frail.

Best of all is God is with us,
life goes on and needs are met,
God is strongest in our weakness.
Love renews, will not forget.

Best of all is God is with us,
hearts are challenged, strangely warmed,
faith is deepened, courage strengthened,
grace received and hope reformed.

Best of all is God is with us,
in our joy and through our pain,
till that final acclamation:
'life is Christ, but death is gain'.

Best of all is God is with us
as we scale eternal heights,
love grows stronger, undiminished;
earth grows dim by heaven's lights.

Tune:    Chapel Brae
Metre:   8.7.8.7

# Tune: Chapel Brae

Evelyn F. Abbott (1927- )

1. Best of all is God is with us, God will hold and ne - ver fail.

Keep that truth when storms are ra - ging, God re - mains though faith is frail.

# Blessings

In the morning call to caring, God will enable you.
In the day-long attendance, God will sustain you.
In the evening of weariness, God will hold and strengthen you.
In the nightwatch of waiting, God is beside you.


When weariness cries out for an end to suffering, God is listening to you.
When fear is like a smothering blanket, God will wrap his care around you.
When life is slipping away, God is walking each step of the journey with you.
When the door closes on this life, God is there to open the way to what lies ahead.

# Death of family members
## *a death in the family*

*People say that the death of a child of whatever age is the most difficult death to cope with. They are right. Naturally, children are supposed to outlive their parents. There is something intrinsically unnatural about the death of a child. Our parents have invested in us biologically, and probably in many other ways. We invest in our children and they are a continuation of ourselves. So losing a child is like experiencing a death of part of yourself. This is something you never 'get over.' You will always remember. And in different ways people learn to cope, to live with the grief and loss.*
*However short the life, there is grief. A mother who experiences a still birth, or an abortion, will grieve. A father will grieve too.*

# They let me hold you in my arms

They let me hold you in my arms,
still aching from your birth,
so limp, I loved you, love you still,
so full of human worth.
For all those months I'd felt you grow,
so conscious of your weight;
anticipated all we'd share.
Did God control your fate?

O God, what is the sense of this,
this wasted, longed for life?
What is the reason, scheme or plan
that needs this pain and strife?
A part of me was torn away,
and all my hope is gone.
The colours fade, the songs are flat,
the endless days go on.

O help me God, if God you are,
to live beyond this pain;
and, not forgetting he was born,
to learn to live again.

# Unbearable loss

O God, the pain of this loss is unbearable.
Our child. Such a small child.
So little a life.
Why such a brief joy? All the anticipation,
the hopes, the plans, the love that was
immediate and overwhelming, but now
is lost.
Why did you allow us to experience such
joy, only to snatch it away leaving
agonizing pain?
This situation is beyond understanding.
Sometimes, even beyond tears.
Hold us when we cry. Understand our
bleak emptiness.
Help us to cope with learning to live again,
without the promise of the new future
we had planned.

*Thoughtlessly, people sometimes greet a bereaved parent with the expectation that they might have more children; that they have other children; that they can take delight in the grandchildren of a nephew or niece. All of these things are true and can be immensely fulfilling. They can also be monstrously hurtful. These are gifts to be discovered, not pointed out by others as a possible panacea.*

# This tragedy has seared our lives

This tragedy has seared our lives
and care seems pointless, love feels dead,
a deep and darkening shroud arrives
and everything is filled with dread.

We cannot face the dawning day,
the sun will emphasize our grief,
while children's laughter only mocks
and words of faith bring no relief.

We feel alone within a crowd.
O God we need to know your hold
for we have lost all grasp of hope
and grace and joy are frozen cold.

Amid this winter of our life
rekindle love and thaw our hope,
then fan the embers of our faith,
revive our strength and help us cope.

Tune:   Breslau
Metre:  LM

*I threw myself down to the ground and tore at the grass like an animal. I cried with primeval intensity. I plumbed the depth of unimaginable pain. My son was dead. I needed my scream to fill the world, that all the earth could share my agony. I wept inconsolably. I needed to expel my grief. I felt selfish, hurt, angry. I wanted to be heard. I could see no way out.*

*How could the pain be numbed?*

*Sounds melodramatic, but it happened. Losing a child is like having part of you torn out. There is no easy resolution. You don't get back to normal, and you never forget. In time you may learn to cope, to adopt less anti-social behaviour. You may question your faith, or lose it. Only one thing is certain: you will never be the same again.*

# No trite words of benediction take away the pain

No trite words of benediction take away the pain.
No soft words of resurrection bring him back again.
Here beyond your words of comfort, lonely, lost I sit.
While you scatter pearls of wisdom I just feel the grit.
While you talk about your children, watch them come and go,
I will tend a tiny grave and watch the flowers grow.

# We play with children, grasp a sense of wonder

We play with children, grasp a sense of wonder,
then recollection breaks it all asunder,
another child had offered expectation,
that child is dead, we feel no consolation.

We thought that we might grow beyond this season,
that time would bring new hope, provide a reason,
but grief has stayed beyond our fear's prediction,
and joy we share, just feeds the contradiction.

*Death can sometimes be understood. Some causes of death strain our comprehension beyond limits. They seem so devoid of purpose or reason that they test, or even destroy, any sense of faith we have. Progeria is a condition in which children age rapidly and prematurely and die young.*

# Look at the world. What does it say?

Look at the world. What does it say?
It speaks of anger, wrath and death.
A child lies dying in your arms,
another breathes a rasping breath.

Jesus is Lord? You jest, of course?
As children age before their time,
as parents strain to understand
a life that's lost its sense of time.

What is the purpose you discern
when lives are mangled, trodden down?
The platitudes we cast about
are sharp as any thorny crown.
So much of life denies God's love,
and faith is sorely tested, tried.
If we believe in God at all,
we sometimes think that God has died.

So hold us, help us through this storm,
this life devoid of human hope,
give strength to live through each new day,
God help us when we cannot cope.

*The death of a child can destroy all sense of purpose. It throws pride into perspective. It can change the whole direction of your life.*

# The father's story

People think of me as being wise. Little do they know!
Well I'd done all the exams, I'd got all the qualifications. I knew it all. And I knew that others knew I knew it too! I could command the price.

Of course I was humble – with a due sense of humility. There was no point in pushing it on others. But pride comes before ... and it was some fall. They can't take your learning away from you, of course. Nor the esteem in which others hold you – not unless you really blot your copy book! They don't rescind the qualifications.

No. That wasn't it.

Death was what did it. No, not mine. This is no resurrection appearance! It might be more comfortable if it was.

He died. My only son. Flesh of my flesh. I might as well have died myself for how I felt. None of the wealth or the understanding or the wisdom mattered. They couldn't bring him back. That esteem in which others held me was empty. But because of how they saw me they thought I'd just ride this wave, be untouched by the pain, immune to the grief.

I went back into work. They acted as if nothing had happened. But my heart had been torn out. So I went under. I collapsed. No, not literally. Just went under. I couldn't work. I needed counselling. I, who had often offered that to others, now needed help myself.

The tragedy turned my life upside down. It certainly showed me what matters – and it's not wealth or knowledge.

It's the love of those you love, it's the people that you cherish.  Then, suddenly, they've gone!

I crawled back. I managed to regain my role. I worked my work and did what was expected of me. But there was no joy in it. It was all just bleak and dark and lonely.
There was an echo of a text I remembered, 'nothing in all creation that can separate us from the love', but they're just empty words ... print on paper.

Unless, of course, someone makes them real for you.

So, 'I waited patiently for the Lord';

Well, not so patiently actually. I railed against God, more like. In my own way.

But,
> 'he turned to me and heard my cry.
> He lifted me out of the slimy pit,
> > out of the mud and mire;
> he set my feet on a rock
> > and gave me a firm place to stand.'

Well, it wasn't so much God. But perhaps it was God ... it didn't look like God ... but people don't ... do they?
But, it must have come from God ... there was such compassion ... such healing!
And it was all through people! People God sent?
Yes! I'm sure he sent them.

Because it did happen – for me. He lifted me. I certainly couldn't have done it for myself. But he sent the people who could.

And it was like resurrection! 'Thine be the glory!'
It's still not easy, but it's beginning to be bearable now and it's like getting my life back. I'm not there yet.
I still miss him, of course I miss him.

But it's different now. Nothing can tear him from that love. And I feel it's real too.
> 'He put a new song in my mouth,
> > a hymn of praise to our God'.

I think I'm un-growing.

I'm losing certainty and gaining faith ... I know I'm trusting more.
I'd had too much belief in myself – in my own ability.
Now I know I need to trust God more.

He heard my cry! Even though it was a cry of anger.

Thank you God, thank you and thank you again! A new start, yes! A new start!
Alleluia!!

*Death brings questions and doubts.*

# God has always been good to me

God has always been good to me, so far.
Why has this happened now?
Even to think that 'only the good die young',
    or 'she was too good for this world',
    is so agonizingly hypocritical that I'm
    infuriated that people could ever
    dare to say such things.

But, where is God now?
Why am I suffering like this?
Is it true, what some people think,
    that God is cruel?
Is God there at all?

I've always believed in a loving God.
I want to believe now.
But surely a loving God would not
    allow such pain?
God!
Help me to pray

I'm hurting so much
and my faith is almost non-existent.

Please, God.
Don't desert me now.

Show me you are there. Please.

*A news reporter films a body bag, but a mother sees her child. Platitudes preached from a pulpit can be just as callous.*
*Is there resurrection? Her child is now buried under six feet of soil ...*

# I cannot get my head around

I cannot get my head around
the vastness of the loss
accepted by the God of all,
now hammered to a cross!
I cannot understand the grief
a mother has to bear
when looking at a body bag,
to know her child lies there.

And Mary stands and weeps again,
and God still suffers pain,
but for that mother standing there
such comment seems inane.

So when we preach or speak of Christ
to those who need relief,
God help us empathize with them
that we might know their grief.

*Memories are precious. However sharp to the touch they may be at the moment, hold on to them. Memories can be blown away. Share them, keep them alive. Remember!*

# Remember

You love him. That's why you feel like this.
   That will never change.

Without you he wouldn't have discovered life,
   enjoyed learning, driven you crazy as he
   strained in adolescence to gain his
   independence while needing you more
   than he would admit, or you could know.
And he still needs you, in spite of his death.
In death as in life, he is your child,
   to be remembered with all the love
   you ever had for him,
with all the frustration he brought you,
as well as the joy and privilege of parenthood.
Love him still.
Always love him.
Talk about his birth, his life, his ups and downs.
Talk of success and failure.
Talk of love and frustration.
Talk about him.
And never, never let him go.
He is your son.
He was and is and always will be.
The joyful pain of knowing that will live with
   you forever.
Every day you will picture him,
hear his voice
and ask the unanswerable 'what ifs'
until that point when it registers that,
in spite of all that has happened
nothing, but nothing,
can separate you, or him, from God's love.
Even now you are still a uniquely valued
   child of God.

God hurts with you,
cries with you,
holds you,
enfolds you with love.
And you are safe.
Nothing can harm you anymore.
Your memories are safe and the love in
   which you are held is eternal.
So rest, my child, in that love of God
   that will never,
but never, let you go.

*Sometimes turning to the Bible with imagination can help us. It doesn't take grief away, but it does show us that others have walked along the same paths as ourselves; that there are no easy answers; that life and death can both be very harsh partners for us. And the stories don't answer back, or say 'for me it was like this.' They just stand beside us to comfort, or to share our agony. They are just there. Here we imagine Mary. Jesus has died. His body has been taken from the cross, but not yet buried ...*

# Mary

They let me hold him before they took his body away.

They lifted him so gently and carefully and laid him so that his scourged back and bleeding shoulders rested against the soft fabric of my dress. I could feel the torn flesh weeping through the cloth, spreading and seeping through to my skin.

The thorns, that mockery of a crown, had gone.
Friends had taken them away as quickly as they could, but some had gone so deep they had broken and couldn't be removed and the imprint of that cruel irony was written there in blood.

I held his hands, once strong and skilful, crafting wood in the workshop, using the tools of his trade.
Gentle, trusting hands I'd held through childhood, now mangled by hammer and nails – an executioner's tools.
Healing hands, hands that had helped so many – now broken, the flesh pierced, opened and torn; the bones crushed and splintered.

And had they needed to strike with that spear at the end?
Couldn't they see he was dead already?
Why did they have to put that senseless wound in his side?
What had he done to deserve any of that?
Couldn't they even let his dead body alone?

So, as I cradled his tortured, bloodied head and strand by strand, lifted his tangled hair away from the open wounds above his staring eyes, I raged against the God who gave him to me and then tore him from me in such a violent fashion.

Oh, God! Why did you let this happen?
You could have saved him! You could have warned him! You could have let him escape.
You could have changed their minds before they did this to him.
You had the power – why didn't you use it?

And as I wept and railed at God, my tears washed down over his beloved face and mingled with his blood and I closed his God-forsaken eyes to shut out the desolation I saw there.
At that last moment he'd felt abandoned – even God wasn't listening.

But I would make him listen!

How could he do this to my son? A mother shouldn't have to watch her child die – and die in such agony.
To feel that no one, not God, not his mother, cared what was happening to him!

Because I couldn't touch him. I couldn't help him.
They wouldn't let me near enough to do anything.

Only when it was too late; too late to comfort him; too late for him to feel my touch, to hear my words of love; only then, when it was too late, did they let me come to him.

What kind of a God allows that to happen?
What kind of a God doesn't answer the prayer of a dying man?
What kind of a God promises so much and then allows those promises to die so soon?

They had to take his body from me.

They were so gentle and understanding, those friends, but I didn't want to let him go.
I knew I couldn't do anything for him. Nothing would bring him back.

But still I clung to him, knowing it was useless, desperately longing to show him the love he had needed in those last agonizing moments. Would he ever know how much I wanted to take his place? I should have been the one to die, not him.

I am his mother. I bore him with pain and blood. And when they took his body from me, I felt he had been torn from me again.

But this agony is unbearable and this blood is his, not mine.
How could God take someone so young, so vibrant, so alive?
Oh, God! What have you done?

Now he is gone. There is nothing more I can do. His life is over. My agony and desolation is just beginning.

Dear God! I feel so angry. I wish I could make sense of this! I hope you can! All I can do is weep.

*Not all grieving is straightforward, if any is. Some grieving is covert. Grief sharpens all our feelings. Not all relationships are accepted by society. When death breaks in, how do we grieve? We do need to grieve.*

# I long to grieve with all my heart

I long to grieve with all my heart,
he was the closest one to me;
but there is one who takes my place,
it is her grief the world will see.

Within the coldness of my room
I tear at pillows, scream inside.
Beyond these walls I wear a mask
while others point, and some deride.
They do not understand, the love
that held us through the winter's gloom,
that painted colours in the spring,
that now I share an empty room.

O Lord, you understood the one
who drew you water from a well.
You recognized her chequered life,
but offered love instead of hell.

I'm trapped and yet the love we shared
held beauty and was meant to be.
O God, am I entirely wrong?
O hold me fast and comfort me.

*Sometimes there is no body ...*

# The 'not knowing'

It's the 'not knowing' that's so hard. Logically she must be dead, I know that. But my mind's not logical. My tears are frozen, but I want to cry. Then, what if there's nothing to cry for? Every ring of the 'phone, knock on the door, fresh email brings hope ... dashed. So I wait through the void of days, the vacuum of a life that used to be filled with little things. The touch of her hand, the sound of her voice, the kiss of her lips ... O God, if I ever needed you, I need you now. Somehow, just somehow, hold me in your love. Help me just to get through another empty day, another night, until tomorrow ... please God ...

*When our parents die we lose people who have, by definition, always been there. They preceded us and all the platitudes in the world about 'good lives' and age do not always assuage the immense loss that we feel.*

# Losing a parent

They've always been there. If they've been healthy and active why should they die? Best friend. Gone. So much to share. So much still to do. And I question the suffering that led to her death, even the need for death at all. And I'm angry, and lonely and lost. Now I have to do things myself. Now I can't delve into mum's experience. Words like, 'a good age', 'a better place', just make me fume. I want her here and now. I want to be able to be cross with her and make up again. I just want to go over again and again all the experiences and times that have built my life, that we shared together. That's all. And I don't want to be without her and don't see why I should. I feel let down. How could she leave me like this? I want to rattle the cage of God.

# I stood among the desolation

I stood among the desolation
of a room frozen for ever
at that instant of death.
No time to clear that cup
of untouched tea.
No hurried signs
of tidying for visitors,
or ordering of papers.

She had been a hoarder.
There was no making sense
of piles of books
and clothes and magazines:
all the clutter and chaos
of seventy-six years.

My cry was genuine.
'Oh, God!
Where do I start?'

The answer was immediate.
The doorbell rang
and on the doorstep
stood an angel
in a pinafore.
My mother's friend.
My personal
faith encourager.

'What can I do?
You need me.'

God's hands
and arms of comfort
embodied.
Just for me.

*Watching someone die is so painful ...*

# I watched the autumn shadows fall

I watched the autumn shadows fall,
the greying of the light,
the quietness, not solitude,
anticipating night;
but not the ending of a day,
the closing of a life,
the staggering breaths that indicate
an ending of this strife.

And I have watched, and I have loved,
the one I held and hold,
in far too little time for me,
grow lined and frail and cold.
This death deferred, this waiting room,
where memories evolve,
is cold and stark, is grim and dark,
and grief will not dissolve.

I watched the autumn shadows fall,
the greying of the light,
the quietness, not solitude,
anticipating night.

# He went to sleep

He went to sleep.
It was so peaceful.
He'd woken to greet me
with his gentle smile –
the spark of life
now dimming in his eyes –
and then he simply fell asleep
and didn't wake up again.

After all that pain,
the God he'd served so faithfully
answered my prayer
for peaceful death.
He simply fell asleep
and woke again with God.

*Scriptures that might be helpful –*
*Luke 2.29-32*

*We anticipate the future, building our expectations on our experience of the past.*

# All my life I've made acquaintances

All my life I've made acquaintances
not friends,
a varied tapestry of faces,
none permanent,
born and dying.
Parents gave me birth,
both now dead.
Child born
and laid to rest.
One human love remains constant,
always constant since we met,
yet even she will die.
And if I survive,
at the ultimate parting of the ways,
I will be alone.
Left again to my earliest memories,
to the rising of the sun
and its setting;
to waxing of the moon
and its waning;
the movement of the waters,
the crashing of the waves,
the constancy of stars;
to the generation of my faith.
In this dynamic patchwork
I find my safety,
lodge securely;
and so,
in death,
I will return again
to the friendly sea
and the sky.

*The loss of a partner can be devastating. This is the person with whom you have lived and shared intimately. Together you may have brought up children. You have been through all the ups and downs, the joys and arguments of life. You relied on each other and life is different and it will never, ever return to 'normal' again. You might, given time, adjust to what is.*
*When my father-in-law died, I wrote this for my mother-in-law.*

# When the life we lived for stumbles

When the life we lived for stumbles,
when our love is torn away;
when our safety shakes and crumbles,
greyness covers every day;
hope and faith seem to evade us
and we cannot even pray;
God be with us in our anguish,
share the pain to which we're prey.

When the morning's dawn is hollow,
and the loneliness we dread
follows through each day of sorrow,
watches over tears we shed;
when we seek within the silence
sounds of life which once we shared,
speak to us, with hope enfold us,
show the love with which Christ cared.

Lift us from the vale of shadows,
raise us to a higher plain,
intercept the doubt that follows
grief and suff'ring, fear and pain.
colours that have lost their brilliance,
Lord, restore and bring to light;
that assured of love's existence
we might break out of the night.

Tune:    Bethany (Henry Smart)
Metre:   8.7.8.7.D

*... and a reflection*

# One half of me has gone

One half of me has gone
and I am totally unbalanced.
I want to lean,
as I have always done,
to feel the comfort
of another alongside me.
But, if I did,
I'd fall.
The one I used to lean upon
has gone
and half of me is missing.
I tell myself I'll cope.
In my imagination
I have lived this day before –
this learning to be alone –
and, in reality, I know
so many who have walked
this desolate way,
this parting from each other
in the finality of death.
But, right now,
I am unbalanced
and afraid
and lost
without the one I loved –
still love –
and leaned upon.

# Silence

The room is still, although the clock ticks on
and noise is filtered by the empty air.
The gate, next door, clicks out a 'welcome home'
and children chatter on their way from school.
The traffic passes in the street outside;
a siren sounds, a police car rushes by.
A child shrieks out in play and calls a friend
and soon a noisy game of football starts.

But in the room these sounds are lost, ignored
by that lone figure spellbound in the chair,
deaf to the living, loving, breathing world;
wrapped in himself and drowned in memories.
Those were the days of laughter and of tears,
when all the house was ringing out with love.
But now, alone, he hears the bitter truth –
the saddest silence is the lonely heart.

# My empty heart

My empty heart
aches with tears.
My empty arms
long to enfold him.
My empty mind
can think of nothing else, but him.
My empty life
lies frighteningly before me.
Loving God,
hold my hand
in this desolate time
for I am afraid
and utterly alone.

# Emptiness

Dear God, this is one of those days when everything around me brings a stark reminder of my loss.
The book, with paper marking the place beyond which nothing will ever be read. That favourite
mug, unused now, but never to be discarded. The biscuits I don't eat, but bought for ...
It's so often the smallest reminders that bring the sudden tears.
I wept when I found that unwashed handkerchief in the pocket of clothes for the charity shop. I
was overwhelmed when I found the birthday card, signed and sealed and ready for my special
day. And when I look over to that chair ...
All those empty spaces! All those unfinished, everyday things!
Oh, God! I wish! I wish ...

Caring God, people tell me that the hurt will fade with time, but that's not how I feel today. Today
is bleak and lonely.
Hold out your arms of love to me, especially at those times when I feel that you're not there. Touch
me with your care and help me to recognize when someone else is doing that on your behalf.
I need you. Now!

# Blessings

Though family life will never be the same,
God will care for you.
Though empty spaces speak of loss,
God will support you.
Though tears come as memories hurt,
God will comfort you.
Though changes demand new ways of coping,
God will guide and hold you.
God knows what you need and will help and bless you.


God holds you through the weeping hours.
God watches through the sleepless nights.
God comes into the lonely room.
God loves you through your time of loss.
God understands and blesses you.

# If only ...

*clinging to faith
and asking questions*

*Even when death is natural we want answers to our questions, the 'whys?' and 'what ifs?' And if we are surrounded by people who have perhaps not grieved, they won't necessarily understand why we are like we are. We are the ones who have our backs against the wall.*

# O for a faith, a simple faith

O for a faith, a simple faith,
that holds against all odds;
but I live in a concrete world,
of humans, not of gods.

Here all the pain is tangible,
and all the grief is real;
and pretty words can't sanitize
the anguish that I feel.

And all your words are platitudes
that will not recognize
the stark reality of life
they cover or disguise.

O for a faith, a simple faith,
that, tempered in the fire,
has strength to hold through pain and grief,
that's all that I require.

Tune:   Windsor
Metre:   CM

# Tune: Windsor

Damon's *Psalmes*, 1591

1. O for a faith, a sim-ple faith, that holds a-gainst all odds;

but I live in a con-crete world, of hu-mans, not of gods.

*When human help is inappropriate, or absent altogether, we turn to God. Many a true prayer has been wrung out of the grief of those who thought they believed least.*

# Father God

Father God!
What a comfort there is in those words.
You don't know how much I need a
    loving father right now.
But then you do, don't you?
    That's the whole point!
You know when I feel low and sad
    and need a shoulder to cry on.
You know when everything around seems
    grey and heavy and hostile.
You know all about misunderstanding and
    betrayal and isolation.
You understand the dark night of the soul.

Because you became like me and you
    went through it all too.

Thank you, Father,
That Jesus made it very clear that you
    suffer with us.
Please stand by me,
so that one day I will see the light
    shining again.

# God of innocence and beauty

God of innocence and beauty,
God of death and deep despair,
God, through tears of desolation
I am crying, are you there?

God of penetrating wisdom
reaching pain within my soul;
can you feel, then reach much deeper,
offer love to make me whole?

God of steadfast loving kindness,
God the grounding of my soul,
God your word informs my knowing.
Give me grace and make me whole.

Tune:    Love divine (Stainer)
Metre    8.7.8.7

*Scriptures that might be helpful –*
*Isaiah 43.1*

# O God, the memories are so painful

O God, the memories are so painful.
If only I could have helped.
If only I could have shown him the depth of my love.
If only he could have known ...

O God, if anyone understands the anguish of love and loss, you do.
You watched your son die.
You saw his agony.
You heard his cry of despair and desolation.
You knew that his death was inevitable,
but that it was not the end.

When my questions lead me nowhere and my regrets are futile, help me to remember that you
	know the depths of my pain and that you walk with me through the dark days.
For I cannot do this on my own.

*After the birth of Jesus, Joseph disappeared from the scene. The most widely held tradition is that he was older than Mary and had died before Jesus came to the cross. But there is one tradition that has Jesus dying while Joseph was still alive. In short, we don't know.*

*But if Joseph was alive, and if he disappears from the gospel record because he simply wasn't around to be included, he begins to provide a model for the estranged parent at the time of death. Let imagination tell the story ...*

# The unseen Joseph

It is his hands that I'll remember.

How could I forget them?

Years ago I knew them as well as I knew my own. But, in death – O God! – what had they done to him? His hands were torn apart, crushed by the hammer, broken by the nails, then opened even further by the weight of his body hanging from them.

It makes me retch to think of them, but I can't get that sight out of my head.

Those hands were such an important part of my life once.

I remember tiny fingers gripping my thumb as I cuddled and cradled him. Fingers strong enough to lift him, just a little. When I carried him on my shoulders, I felt him tousle my hair. I cradled his hands in mine, guiding the plane, shaving the wood – my finger keeping a saw in its line.

And that mock strength as we arm wrestled, fell from chairs, rolled on the floor.

Then Mary, shouting, reminding me of my age – and of his.

Mary!

It's strange how my thoughts ramble around.

There was always a tension in that relationship.

Yes, I know the stories you've heard. But think of it from my point of view. I loved her and she was vulnerable. She was pregnant. I wasn't going to let her go – I couldn't do that to her.

But the gossips got talking. And there were some very odd happenings – visions and the like. I believed I was doing the right thing at the time, but it all got to be too much.

I suppose it came to a head that day in the temple when Jesus was twelve. 'Didn't you know I'd be about my Father's business' he said.

Father's business indeed!

My business was carpentry and you don't learn about that by sitting in front of teachers in the temple!

Mary said nothing and when I realized why, I felt like a fool. But, by then, I thought of myself as his real father and it was a shock to recognize that Jesus would not always be following in my footsteps.

After that, things were never quite the same again.

Jesus did learn the carpentry trade and he was good at it, but as time went by I sank more and more into the background. So it was no real surprise when I left the family, though my first excuse was that I needed to get work nearer to the city.

Then I just didn't go back. I regret it – of course I do! But the gap between us widened so much over the years that it got to the point where there was no going back.

Then I heard that he was in Jerusalem.

My own flesh and blood. My son.

I know, I know, I'd left them, but do you think I didn't miss him?

So I went to the temple and that was a strange experience.

I kept my distance and made sure I was out of sight. But I heard what he was saying, saw what he was doing – and it was so damned inflammatory. He didn't care who he offended, or what danger he was making for himself. So, when I heard he'd been arrested, I wasn't surprised, although I was terrified on his behalf.

I knew the city well by now and got into that courtyard where Peter was sitting, waiting. It was brave of him to go there at all, but a fat lot of support he turned out to be. My son knew that too – I saw the look he gave Peter – and Peter just ran away in tears.

Then the crowds turned against Jesus and jeered at him. Infiltrators got among them and suddenly everyone was shouting for the release of a prisoner. But they didn't want Jesus, so it was Barabbas that walked.

I could see what was coming and it tore at my heart.

I can remember it all.

I wanted to help, but not enough to risk my life. What good would that do?

So I pulled my cloak up round me, because I felt colder than the night air itself. I was chilled with fear, I suppose, and the cloak did no good at all, except to hide me from anyone who might recognize me.

Then I followed at the back of the crowd, but I kept my distance.

It didn't stop me hearing the nails, the hammers, the ringing timber. It was an ironic and cruel death for a carpenter's son.

At a distance, I watched. I even caught the shadow of his cross passing across my hands. Then I saw his hands again – and under that darkened sky I was suddenly back in that stable. Tiny, tiny fingers grasping my thumb – but now they were hammered against splintered wood.

At that point I wanted to hold him so desperately, but it was too late. All I have is just memories and remorse for company.

As I carried him to Mary, for her to hold, no one knew who I was.

As I lifted his pierced, broken body they did not see beyond this workman's cloak. They didn't see the tears. They didn't see me fold my hand round his, massaging those once tiny fingers – vainly trying to fill them with life again.

No one saw that.

And it is his hands that I remember.

*Holding on to faith and hope is not easy. Sometimes it seems impossible. Then, like Jesus on the cross, we may echo the Psalmist crying out in despair (Psalm 22 for instance). There is nothing wrong in this. If we feel forsaken and bereft, then we can and should cry out to God about it.*

# In the testing, when we're hurting

In the testing, when we're hurting,
when the waters drown our hope;
when the fire consumes conviction,
when we've lost the strength to cope;

when the prayer that fear rips from us
has a hollow, empty sound;
when we look to God for comfort,
yet that grace cannot be found;

like the Christ, who hung despairing,
we're forsaken and alone;
and our cry of hopeless horror
finds an echo in his own.

Jesus died, the temple's curtain
sundered as the sky turned dark.
In our darkness, still despairing,
see God's action: simple, stark;

nature's expectation vanquished;
life and love restored, complete.
Working through the pain we suffer
hope and joy renewed, replete.

Tune: All for Jesus (Stainer)
Metre: 8.7.8.7

# We pray for those whose relationship with you feels uncertain

We pray for those whose relationship with you feels uncertain. We ask your blessing on those whose faith is faltering – and especially for those who feel that recent events have undermined their trust in you. Life is not easy, and sometimes doubts are overwhelming. Communication with you seems so broken that prayer feels like an empty activity. Help us, Lord, to fight our way through, holding on to you until the morning comes, till we learn that you have always been with us and will never let us go.

# Oh, why is life cut short like this?

Oh, why is life cut short like this?
It feels that love has been defied.
And 'God' makes little sense at all
when grace and hope have been denied.

God's will did not bring this about,
this suffering, this early death.
To speak like that is blasphemous,
denying God's life-giving breath.

Is God found here in all this pain,
a partner in our loss and grief?
Does God relive Christ's dark despair,
to hold us through our unbelief.

Faith seems to say that God is here,
yet wrung with grief and sharing tears.
This God is not remote or lost,
but stands with us and shares our fears.

Hold on and when you cannot hold,
reach out your fists for God to grasp.
You never fall beyond God's care.
God's grace will live, God's love will last.

Tune:    Herongate
Metre:   LM

# Ashes of memory

Ashes of memory,
all that matters is past
and the past is receding
and there is no point anymore.

Life goes on.

But I don't want to.
No one understands.
They say they listen
but they don't hear.
If they did
they'd know why I feel so helpless,

so hopeless.

*The feeling of anger when someone dies is very common. That anger can be directed at other people who, in our eyes, are responsible for the death that is causing us to grieve. We might take our anger out on an inanimate object, beating a pillow, perhaps breaking crockery or worse. We might be angry with ourselves, blaming ourselves for what has happened. Depression and suicide can be symptoms of this anger.*

# When in grief and filled with anger

When in grief and filled with anger,
lashing out and fired by spite,
in confusion we are startled
by aggression at its height,
quell our temper, sap our vengeance,
help untangle wrong and right.

Every one of us is human,
with our share of pain and grief,
filled with passion, stressed by feelings,
so we find that our belief
fuels our doubting of the Godhead
who could love and bring relief.

As we face a new day dawning
raze the hatred we would fan,
offer undeserved forgiveness
to each woman, to each man,
that together we may function,
fit our purpose in your plan.

Tune: New Malden (McCarthy)
Metre: 8.7.8.7.8.7

*In the desolation we cry out to he held, to be comforted ...*

# God hold us, enfold us, through desolate loss

God, hold us, enfold us, through desolate loss.
The sign of your love is your own empty cross.
The shock and the anger, the hopeless despair
are echoes of Calvary. God, meet us there!

God, hold us, enfold us, through long empty days,
when living is pointless, a meaningless maze.
We need you to listen to raging and tears,
to anguish and doubt, to remorse and to fears.

God, hold us, enfold us, by friends who can share
our sorrow and pain with compassionate care.
By their words, you speak out your loving
   concerns.
They hold us for you, while the tide of grief turns.

God, hold us, enfold us, till weeping has passed;
when flickering hope parts the shadows at last.
One step at a time you will help us to move
to face new horizons, held safe in your love.

Tune: God hold us (June Baker)
Metre: 11.11.11.11

# Tune: God hold us

June Baker (1936- )

God, hold us, en - fold us, thro' des - o - late loss. _____ The sign of your love is your own emp - ty cross. The shock and the ang - er, the hope-less des - pair _____ are ech-oes of Cal - va - ry, God, meet us there.

*Hopefully, we are ultimately able to move through the anger, not burying it, but addressing it and finding new hope ...*

# Now is the time to sing of hurt

Now is the time to sing of hurt,
the pain we hold within,
the damaged psyche, faulted soul,
the dominance of sin.

Now is the time to sound the depths
of sacrificial love,
to feel the covenant of care
that holds like hand in glove.

Now is the time to grasp the hope
that understands our pain,
that moves us on beyond our hurt,
so we can love again.

Tune:   Crimond
Metre:   CM

*At the end of the day, perhaps we just need to live with what might have been and with so many questions unanswered. When we can, we just need to let go and accept that things are as they are. We cannot put the clock back.*

# If only ...

If only I had gone to his room that morning ...
If only I'd insisted on her seeing a doctor ...
If only we hadn't quarrelled on the day of his accident ...
If only she'd been delayed and hadn't caught that train ...
If only I'd told him how much I loved him ...
If only she hadn't insisted on driving ...
If only he'd stopped smoking earlier ...
If only she hadn't had that injection ...
If only I'd been there ...

O God, the 'if only' questions are impossible to answer.
They make no difference to what has happened.
Death has ended the relationship and all the questions are suspended in time, with no resolution.
Teach me how to deal with them, even though it will not be an easy process.
Help me to recognize my inability to change things and to learn from this experience,
    so that I can make a difference in the future.
Guide me through this despair and bewilderment on to acceptance and self-knowledge.
Hold me safely, as I begin to turn my life into this new direction and to face the reality
    of the future.

# Blessings

When it's too late to say, 'I love you';
when it's too late to say, 'Sorry';
when it's too late to make that telephone call;
when it's too late to visit;
when it's too late to give a warning;
when it's too late to notice pain;
when it's too late to forgive, or to be forgiven,
God takes your guilt,
God takes your regrets,
God takes your sorrow
and holds you with loving care
and listens.

God reaches through doubt to offer understanding.
God reaches through pain to offer healing.
God reaches through anger to offer calm.
God reaches through questions, absorbing our frustration.
God offers blessings when we are able to receive them.

# The funeral

*Amid all the questions and our anger, loss and grief, we are asked to address practical things. We meet undertakers, collect death certificates, plan a funeral. People cope with these practicalities differently. For some they are a helpful distraction, for others they are the last practical thing they can do for someone they have loved. For others there is a sense of something to be 'got over.' Yet others find this to be a helpful and necessary part of coming to terms with a death. Imagining how Mary Magdalene could have felt when Jesus died, might give us a story to help us find our way through these muddled feelings.*

# Mary Magdalene

What do I do now?

Dear God, I wish I could stop crying, but I can't. Every time I look at that place where they killed him – and I see the blood and the cross and ... I don't know what to do. What will we do without him? How will we go on?
We're all so lost and I don't know where to turn. But one of us has to take some practical steps.

Come on, Mary. Pull yourself together. Dry your tears. Think! What would he want you to do?

Just at the moment, his mother is being cared for. At least people can guess how she must be feeling and they're surrounding her and supporting her. So that's one thing less to worry about. But, I've got to do something. I always have!

Ever since Jesus got rid of those evil things from my life, I've dedicated myself to looking after him and his followers, so that they could get on with the important work. What else could I do?

You wouldn't believe the way my life has changed since that healing happened. There's no way I could ever really repay that debt to him. He made me into a new woman; the least I could do was to try to make his life a little easier and more comfortable. Make sure he had some quietness occasionally and some care and concern lavished on him, instead of him giving out all the time. Because the men didn't seem to think about that. They were always bringing people to him when it was obvious that he needed to rest. And I've never met such a group for being careless about food and finding places to sleep. They never did any advance planning.
So we women got together to make sure they were all right. Women are usually more practical in that way. We're used to it – and it's expected of us.
And, today, we've certainly proved our loyalty.
Where have all the men gone? Nearly all of them ran away. I know it's easier for us because no one cares about women being here, but you'd have thought some of them would have been brave enough ...
Oh, dear God, I'm going to cry again. Stop it, Mary! Think what to do next!

We must find out where they're taking him for burial.

There isn't time for the oils and spices now. We'll have to go after the Sabbath. But we'll need to know where the grave is.

At least he'll have a proper grave. That rich man from Arimathea, Joseph, has given up his own tomb, thank God. So Jesus will have a decent burial. But we'll have to follow, if we want to find it later. Salome will come with me.

But what will happen after that? Where will we go? What will we do?

Our whole lives were wrapped up in Jesus and his life. Now it's all gone. No future. No hope!

Oh, God, why didn't you help us to stop him coming here?

He wouldn't listen to us. We knew he was walking straight into danger. But he just kept on heading for Jerusalem.

And then, all this! Plotting and treachery and cruelty. Did you see the state he was in even before they started hammering in the nails?

No! Don't think! Do something. Something practical. Anything.

I know one thing I'd like to do. I'd like to spit in the face of that priest over there – the one who's actually smiling to himself.

The hypocrite! No doubt he'll think he's won a great victory today. Why were they so scared of such an innocent man? Couldn't they see all the good he was doing?

No, they couldn't! All they could see was that he was undermining their power base.

But there was no need to have him killed in that barbaric way.

Yet Jesus did warn us about them.

Oh, look, the burial party is moving now. Carrying his tortured, wretched body. Disposing of the man we all loved so much.

Look at the state his mother is in. How can she bear the anguish?

And that workman just behind her – even he is showing some respect. I think he's actually weeping too.

We must follow!

Salome! Come!

If we can do nothing else for him now, at least we can anoint his body after the Sabbath. But we need to know where he is, so we can find him when we come to say our final goodbyes.

Wait! Wait for us!

*At a funeral many things go unsaid ...*

# This is the place

This is the place
where death meets life,
where sorrow is present,
where hard questions are asked
and not always answered.

This is the place
where pain is felt,
where partings are made real,
where holy words
can ring empty and hollow.

This is the place
where we ask, 'Why?'
Where we cry, 'What now?'
Where God is near,
or feels so far away.

This is the place
where emotions are mixed,
where tears are shed,
where memories return
of brighter yesterdays.

This is the place
where God says, 'I know.'
Where God says, 'I am here.'
Where God sheds a tear
along with us.

This is the place
where God understands,
where God stands and waits,
where Jesus says,
'I went through it.'

This is the place
where Easter is hope,
where eternity is God,
where each ending
becomes a beginning.

This is the place
where God is all around
and very much alive
because we need him
here in this place.

*There are many liturgies for funerals available in denominational books. For the most part the words of these are determined by the denomination and reflect that denomination's belief. For many, both within and on the fringe of the church, these orders of service make little, if any, sense. The following is offered as an alternative. Traditional words, for instance those of the committal, could still be inserted from readily available sources.*

# An order of service for a funeral

*Call to remembrance*

Here in the presence of death, God is with us.

We have come here today to remember N
to give thanks for him/her, to try to find some
comfort, some help to bear our loss.
We feel numb or angry, helpless or lost.
We need space and time to grieve and to
remember. Some of us need silence, quiet,
to be alone. Others need company
and conversation.
There is no right or wrong way to feel when
someone dies. God can cope with all these
things, so let us share our feelings with God.
Let us pray:

In our vulnerability and loss help us to
hold one another in love.
Like a father, strengthen us.
Like a mother, comfort us.
Enable our tears. Hear our sighs.
Help us to live through our doubt.
Teach us the truth that the darkness has
never overcome the light of your love.
Help us to care for each other and to love
each other through this grief. Amen

And now, O God, remind us of the faith that
has brought encouragement and reassurance
to your people over the years:

*Appropriate Scripture(s): Ecclesiastes 3.1-8;
Psalm 23; Psalm 121; Luke 12.22-31; John
14.1-3, 27; Romans 8.35, 37-39.*

These words speak of the experience of people
in the past. We may or may not be able to
make them our own. They may sound hollow
or irrelevant. Come back to them again, in a
month, in a year. Perhaps then they'll make
sense. What is sure, is that the love of which
the Bible speaks is made real when we,
humanly, love each other. We become
channels, instruments, of God's love.

*A remembrance – A tribute to the deceased*

Let us remember N You know N
Picture him/her in your mind's eyes.
Thumb through the photographs of your
memory, run again the film of the life you
shared. Remember the sunshine and the rain,
the laughter and the tears, all that made N
unique and special, all that continues to keep
him/her special for you now.

*Silence*

We remember N
We thank you for him/her.
We are grateful for all he/she has meant to us.
Help us to set aside the time when things went
wrong, for we are all human and make mistakes.
Help us to keep him/her alive by seeking to do
the good things that he/she did, to repeat to each
other kind words found on his/her lips.
We are thankful because our lives are different
because we have known him/her.
We will never be the same again.

**All:   The Lord's Prayer**

Until N died we have been able to do things with
him/her and for him/her. That is no longer
possible. We do not know what exists beyond this
life, but Christians believe that those who die are
held in God's love. Affirm that, if you can, by
sharing in this prayer:

**All:   We thank you, God, for N whose life we
        have shared. We commend him/her to you.
        Enfold him/her in your love, keep him/her
        in your care, now and always. Amen.**

*At this point a prayer of blessing may be said if
the committal is not to take place immediately:*

**All:   Go with us God, as we go together from
        this place. Walk with us always and
        wherever we go we ask that you will never
        leave us or forsake us.**

*At the graveside or crematorium these words
may be said. Otherwise the service proceeds
straight to the committal.*

We continue our remembrance of N
Let us pray:

In the pain and joy of remembrance you have
been with us, O God. At this point of leaving stay
with us still. Amen

*The committal*

We have seen and known N and now we hand
him/her back to you. You created him/her. As we
lay his/her body to rest receive him/her as your
own. Amen.

And now let us pray for each other.

Parent God, you feel our pain and cry with us.
You understand what it feels like to be lost and
forsaken. Help us, as you understand our needs.
And as we are comforted, help us to comfort one
another. One day, if not now, may we be able to
affirm that as we grieved, even at the lowest
point, we were not separated from your love, for
we found it in neighbour and friend, sister and
brother, parent and child.
And may that same love surround us and bless us,
protect us and strengthen us, to the end of this
day and even forever more. Amen.

The peace of God which is beyond our
understanding keep us always in the love of God.
And the blessing of God the Creator, the
compassion of Jesus and the comfort of the Holy
Spirit remain with us and with those we love,
both living and dead, this day and evermore.
Amen.

*Hymns for funerals are often those we know well, or those that were appreciated by the person who has died. Other hymns and poems can sometimes speak profoundly to our situation. A few are offered here. Most of the tunes are readily available; many are well-known.*

# Here in this place we meet with you in sorrow

Here in this place we meet with you in sorrow,
our hearts and minds with memories are filled.
We fear to face our emptiness tomorrow,
when thoughts are sad and many tears are spilled.
And yet we know Lord, you have told us clearly
that where you are, there also we will be.
You came to bring a hope of life eternal,
a promise of a future joy we cannot see.

Here in this place we gather in thanksgiving
for all we shared, the joyful days gone by;
for those we love, our chosen life's companions
and those who care and hold us when we cry.
And Lord, we know that you will take the future,
that you will walk beside us in the way
to take us on, to make a new beginning,
to comfort, guide and keep us as we face each day.

Tune:    Londonderry Air
Metre:   Irregular

# O rest in peace at last, and lie contented

O rest in peace at last, and lie contented,
it's finished now, the task you came to do;
life's thrusting power has finally relented,
the summit gained where God makes
    all things new.

Then should we mourn, for God has
    held you safely?
We do not doubt that Christ's care will remain.
the peace that Jesus promised now awaits you,
an end to tears, an end to grief and pain.

O rise in expectation at that promise,
God works for good in what we greet as ill;
have faith, my friend, a greater gift awaits us
than all our hopes of heaven could fulfil.

We look with eyes constrained by human
    knowledge,
but God works out of view of human sight;
so rest in hope, the Spirit give you courage,
that you might face the dazzle of God's light!

Tune:    Stewardship or O perfect love
Metre:    11.10.11.10

# As blood of youth or age

As blood of youth or age
returns to earth from whence it came,
help us to grasp that love remains
and name your name.

The pain of grief is met
and, though each grief is not the same,
help us to grasp that love remains
and name your name.

While walking from the grave
with tears, release, with fault or blame,
help us to grasp that love remains
and name your name.

Our life is changed by death,
sometimes we stagger, miss our aim.
Help us to grasp that love remains
and name your name.

A thousand ages pass,
yet still you magnify our claim
that through our grief your love remains.
We name your name.

Tune:    As blood of youth (June Baker)
Metre:    6.8.8.4

*Scriptures that might be helpful –*
*Psalm 90.4; 121*

# Tune: As blood of youth

June Baker (1936- )

As blood of youth or age re-turns to earth from whence it came,

help us to grasp that love re-mains and name your name.

*We may sing but we will also pray. Some of the most sincere and profound prayers come at the time of grief as we struggle with 'what is'.*

# We pray for people

We pray for people who are battling with grief and especially for those we know who have recently been bereaved. In these situations there is often anger, as well as sorrow; regret, bewilderment, fear and an aching hole filled only with tears. Jesus, you wept at the death of a friend and we weep too. But in the battle to cope there are also breathing spaces. Memories, which lighten the day, even though hearts are sad; caring people who reach out in sympathy and understanding; your breath of love whispering through the struggle. Bless those who mourn, Lord, and comfort them.

# God gave us cause to sing

God gave us cause to sing
our songs of praise ran high,
but that was in another time,
now darkness clouds the sky.

The tears that we will cry,
the shroud of grief we wear,
are evidence of sundered love,
of all we have to bear.

As Mary wept for Christ,
while grief was sharp and raw,
so now we feel akin with her
through all we felt, and saw.

God sow a seed of hope,
and give us, through your grace,
the merest essence of your love
to resurrect our faith.

Tune:    Franconia
Metre:  SM

# Memorial

There is no grave
on which to place
and replace flowers,
brightening a corner
with your memory.
No headstone keeps your name
permanent in chiselled marble.
No grassy mound
to weed or water
for conscience sake,
or to fulfil
the local graveyard byelaws.

It was a conscious choice,
not to identify you
with a patch of earth.

For now you cannot be confined.
Your spirit soars,
free from pain,
in every breeze that blows.
Your soul is safe
with the God
whose existence
you denied and doubted,
or affirmed in faith,
in testing stages on your road.

And we who knew you,
see you in the soaring birds,
the crashing waves,
the towering trees you loved
and taught us love of them.
Your memorial is your delight in life,
that brightened our days
and cannot be forgotten.

*People remember in different ways. Some
need memorials and places. Others don't.
For some there is no possibility of a resting
place for the dead. No cremation. No body.
There is no right way to remember.*

# The grave

I know she is not there –
not really.
That plot of earth
could not contain
someone so full of life.
Yet, every time
I take the flowers,
pull out the weeds,
smooth the rough gravel
and see the name
etched in the stone –
every time,
I cannot help myself –
I talk to her.
This place becomes a focus
for the memory.
Flowers she will never
see, or smell,
are still an offering
of love;
testimony to the truth
that she will never die
while I live on;
witness to the world
that here lies someone
who was worth the loving.
A loving that will never end
for me.

*Through all of this we need human care and, if we can be open to it, the sense of the presence of God can help.*

# Blessings

May God bless you and be with you in this time of deep sorrow.
In the tears of others, know that he weeps with you.
In the touch of others, know that his arms are holding you.
In the practical work of others, know that he is helping you to cope from day to day.
In the words of others, know that he is speaking to you.
In the prayers of others, know that he hears you.

And in the desolation of this time, know that by each tear, touch, act, word and prayer, others are bringing God's love to you to filter into those empty spaces with his compassion and understanding.


The God who sees our tears;
the God who knows our pain;
the God who understands our emptiness
will be with us as we go now,
and as we work through our grief.


God will bless you at this time of parting,
God will hold you through this time of changing.
God will strengthen you for new beginnings.
God will be with you always to help and sustain you,
for the love of God is everlasting.

# Help me!

*for times when we need
to be cared for –
tracing paths of grief*

*Caring and receiving care are not easy things to do. In the midst of grief many people struggle to retain their dignity, their independence, their self-sufficiency. Others want to help, but don't know what to do. How do you get inside another's grief so that the help you offer is appropriate? There are no easy answers.*

# Caring God

Caring God, your heart goes out to those who suffer
and we must reach out too.

But it is not an easy thing to get alongside someone
and feel their suffering with them.
It takes endless patience and time and energy
and we cannot always sustain the effort.

Keep us loving beyond the limits that we believe are possible,
for your care goes further than we can ever imagine
into the darkest places of suffering, grief and despair.

*We need God's care ourselves, but more often than not we experience it through people. Jesus showed that our ideas of God need not be remote or mysterious. We can see Christ in others and be as Christ to them if we have the courage, the audacity. All it takes is the right word, or no word at all. Just being there is often enough.*

# Deepest mystery of passion

Deepest mystery of passion,
far beyond what we can see,
human sense that God is closer
than our breath can ever be.

Christ, exemplar of compassion,
sensed the need in those he saw,
we, who follow in his footsteps,
pledge to make each pain less raw.

Spirit, we would heed your prompting,
moving us to act with grace,
we would emulate Messiah,
mirror love, your human face.

Tune: Cross of Jesus (Stainer)
Metre: 8.7.8.7

*When we try to offer care the most important, and perhaps the most difficult, thing is to be sensitive. When we are, we are more likely to offer the care that someone needs and wants, and not the care we think they need.*

# God of all our senses

God of all our senses, so many people were touched by your love through the hands of Jesus as he
  healed and helped them in his lifetime.
A blind man felt spittle on his eyelids.
A leper felt long-forgotten human connection.
A young girl was given new life as Jesus helped her to her feet.
A woman was healed as she reached out in desperation for his robe.
We sometimes forget what healing power there can be in the sense of touch.

Loving God, we ask a special blessing on those who never feel the friendly touch of someone who
  cares for them –
  those who live alone and are anxious about making contact with others;
  those who suffer physical abuse from people they should be able to trust;
  those who keep themselves apart and have forgotten how to be friendly;
  those who can only respond to others with distrust and anger;
  those whose relationship with their partner is breaking down,
  and especially those who once enjoyed a close, loving relationship with a partner who has now
  died, for they have known the everyday warmth of love and face a special emptiness.

Healing God, touch the lives of those suffering from anxiety, abuse, isolation, anger, broken
  relationships or bereavement.
Teach us to know when it would be appropriate to offer a hand to shake or hold, or the eye contact
  that signifies trust.
We are sometimes too wary of reaching out to offer your hand of healing.
Help us to imagine ourselves into the other person's shoes, so that with your guidance we can offer
  patience, friendship and a genuine loving concern to all who need your care.

*Jesus taught that our neighbour, the one for whom we should care, is simply the person for whom we can care.*

# In times of crisis when we act

In times of crisis when we act
without a thought of self, or fear;
when all that matters is the love
that meets another's crying need,
the love of God prevails, draws near.

To every person, young or old,
we reach with hands of boundless hope;
not knowing where to find the strength,
we struggle through discord, distrust,
with God's unbound resource, we cope.

We circle all the world with care,
the dance and song are intertwined,
the proud gavotte, the tango's pulse,
the lieder's warp, the ballad's weft,
conjoined with God we're wined and dined.

Tune:    Pachelbel
Metre:   88.88.8

# Tune: Pachelbel

1. In times of cris - is when we act with - out a thought of self, or fear; when all that mat - ters is the love that meets a - no - ther's cry - ing need, the love of God pre - vails, draws near.

# Loving spirit kindly lead us

Loving spirit kindly lead us
to a future way;
open doors, protect yet drive us,
give us words to say,
give us words to say.

Give us words or welcome silence,
energize our dance,
offer space and quiet comfort,
give the means and chance,
give the means and chance.

Join our hands, the future beckons,
then beyond our pain,
strengthened by your loving spirit,
help us start again,
help us start again.

Tune:   Loving spirit (June Baker)
Metre:  8.5.8.5.5

# Tune: Loving spirit

June Baker (1936- )

Lov-ing spi-rit, kind-ly lead us to a fut-ure way; ___ op-en doors, pro-

tect yet drive us, give us words to say, ___ give us words to say.

*Every grief is different. And until we begin to grieve
we do not know how we will grieve ...*

# Grief traces paths

*It is impossible to go beyond God's care.*

# Wherever you go

Wherever you go let the love of God hold you,
for nothing can take you where love
    cannot reach.
That love is not bounded by time or
    by distance,
describing such love is beyond human speech.

Today or tomorrow, God's love will not falter,
it's timeless, it's endless, it's warm as the sun;
refreshing as rain falling soft in the morning,
more sure than the tracks where the stars
    soar and run.

Yet while love transcends all the worlds
    in the cosmos,
this love is made real when a hand folds a hand,
it's held in the memory of words and of silence,
the look of an eye that says, 'I understand'.

So go in God's grace, in the power and
    the presence
of love you have known that will not loose
    its hold;
and nowhere you travel, through time or
    through distance
will take you where love cannot care or enfold.

Tune:    St Catherine's Court
Metre:  12.11.12.11

Grief traces paths like walkers over grass.
One takes the way well-trodden,
worn and dry,
compacted by the countless tramping feet
into a hard, bare place.
Another takes soft, solitary steps
deep into clinging grass,
leaving a trail of staggering footprints
soon to be erased by time.

And no one knows which way
until that point of entry
to the field of pain.

*There are times when we do not know what to pray. There are times when we simply cannot pray. 'Likewise the Spirit helps us in our weakness; for we do not know how to pray as we ought, but that very Spirit intercedes with sighs too deep for words' (Romans 8.26).*

# Listening God, you hear us when we cannot speak

Listening God, you hear us when we cannot speak,
when despair and turmoil leaves us faint and weak.
In love you call us back to you again
and your grace reminds us how you feel our pain.

Searching God, you find us when we go astray,
as self-centred living takes us from your way.
In love you seek us, show us what we've lost,
and your tears remind us what forgiveness cost.

Suffering God, you lift us from our deepest grief,
when emotion blinds us to our own belief.
In love you touch us with your nail-torn hand
and your wounds remind us why you understand.

Risen God, you show us love too strong for death.
Evil deeds defeated by your living breath.
In love you teach us never to despair,
your new life reminds us, hope is always there.

Tune:   Noel Nouvelet
Metre:   11.11.10.11

*We think that we know what we need in order to cope with all our feelings. Sometimes we crave solitude. Sometimes loneliness is just too much.*

# Solitude

Just when I get a moment to myself
the phone rings
and I hear the voice
I know so well.
I also know
that time will soon be flying.

But loneliness,
not an issue for me,
is hard for her –
and keeping me a little longer
on the line
puts off the moment
of the single cup of tea
and listless
staring at the television set.

Solitude is not a state
wished for by everyone.

*Though my mother died some 30 years ago, the sight of a certain flower, a purple pansy, will still bring her to mind. She once did a small watercolour painting of that flower in my child's autograph book. The book is long since gone. The memory still remains. And memories can be a mixed blessing.*

# It seems that, though the phases pass

It seems that, though the phases pass,
faith found and joy regained,
within my being some things last
that give recourse to pain.

*Sometimes the after-shock of phases of our lives that we thought we had dealt with still linger. Grief can heighten their effect. At the time of preparation for a funeral, or on the day itself, we can find ourselves meeting people we thought we wouldn't ever have to see again, let alone relate to in a sensitive and constructive way.*

# O Lord, help me!

O Lord, help me!
So much of the past is coming back to haunt me and that's the last thing I need at this time.
Everything is returning and I don't know how to deal with it.
Relationships aren't easy, even with people you love, and broken relationships happen to everybody, but at times like this you have to face up to the past. And I don't know how I'll do it.
But I'll have to – because of this death.
I'll have to meet some of the people I'd rather not meet. There's no time to put things right now, to say the right words, even to plaster over the cracks. If I say what I think, what I feel, it'll be so unpleasant. He wouldn't have wanted that.
But is it right to put on a front and be dishonest! I'm not even sure that I can.

Lord, in the turmoil of these days, in the depths of my grief, help me to cope with meeting him/her/them. At least, help me not to make things worse because of what I feel.
You're the only one who can give me the strength to try to love even those I do not like. And even if it's only for a short time, until this crisis is over, help me to find new levels of patience and tolerance.
I can't do it alone.
Help me, Lord.

*There is so much pain around grief, which though not physical, is very real. The women who went to the tomb of Jesus on the first Easter Sunday, did not immediately think of resurrection. The empty tomb spoke of a lost or stolen corpse.*

# The sharpened chill, the flower-strewn tomb

The sharpened chill, the flower-strewn tomb,
the early morning light,
the heavy stone had rolled away
the women, scared, took flight.

What happened in those latter days
to loosen fear-tied tongues?
We only know grief turned to joy
and laughter filled their lungs.

Their utter grief was real enough,
the record rings as true,
and only time will tell if grief
can change for me and you.

That is our hope, but faith is hard
to grasp, or reconcile
with all that life has brought our way,
and joy is not our style.

Come to the centre of our pain
and sow the seeds of praise,
that, not denying anything,
your love might calm our days.

Tune:   Amazing grace
Metre:  CM

# Blessings

God, who has held you in the past,
knows your present grief and need
and will guide you through the uncertain future.
Though life has changed,
his love for you goes on.
His blessing is with you.


When living has no purpose,
God cares.
When weeping has no ending,
God comforts.
When loving has no reason,
God understands.
When praying is an effort,
God listens.
When your need for love is overwhelming,
God enfolds and blesses you.

# I can't take it in
*sudden death*

*When we are waiting with someone who is terminally ill we may begin to grieve even before they have died. Death is still sharp and it still hurts. The effect of death is not diminished.*

*When death is sudden, there is no time to prepare. There has been no waiting and probably no signal that the person is going to die. In the middle of our routine, quiet or busy, sleeping through the night, working or relaxing, we are suddenly confronted with the fact that someone is dead. Often the fact will be wrapped up in euphemisms – 'had a seizure', 'gone in her sleep' – and more you could name. One fact presents itself, the person you loved has died and you've got to cope with the consequences, whatever they are.*

# He was only going to the shops

He was only going to the shops.

It was a very ordinary day.

And he used the road that was so familiar to him.

Why then?

Why did he step out into the road without looking?

Why did the car have to be travelling so fast?

Why ...?

But there's no point in constantly asking, 'why?'

It was a stupid thing for him to do. He should have known better. One careless step and his life's gone. And he had so much to live for. But now we'll never know. His future ended in that one careless moment.

Oh God, sometimes I'm angry; sometimes I'm overwhelmed by the pointlessness of it all; sometimes the pain is unbearable.

Hold me when I cry, or when I'm angry and take the weight of it all.

Show me that there is still love in this empty, empty world.

*'He has been involved in a fatal accident.' It doesn't matter how you say that you cannot cover up the fact that someone is dead. But a lot of other information has been communicated as well. The person has been killed as opposed to dying 'naturally'. Potentially, someone might be to blame. The words suggest that the death was violent. Exactly how did it happen? By definition you are not prepared for such a death. Very suddenly you have to come to terms with what has happened with no preparation at all.*

# So death strides on and claims another victim

So death strides on and claims another victim,
another life is ground into the dust;
and all our words are worthless, void and empty,
another coarse betrayal of your trust.

How can we go on passively believing,
how can we stand and watch and not protest?
You've given life, can there be no evasion
of agony and strife, no path to rest?

O God, what is the game that you are playing?
Are we just pieces on some chequered board?
Are you forever deaf to our lamenting,
indifferent to the stress that you accord?

Forgive this doubt, but you have given reason
for us to falter in the path of faith;
we read that you will never fail or alter,
but life feels cold and lonely in this place.

If you have heard, O God, will you not answer
our cries that echo from the dawn of time.
O God, amid this pain and manic laughter,
help us to grasp again our riddled rhyme.

Tune:   Intercessor
Metre:  11.10.11.10

*What we want to remember is sometimes hard to claim. We have no control over what we remember and what we forget. We're left to cope with what lodges in our minds.*

# I will never get that image out of my mind!

I will never get that image out of my mind! It is so vivid. Doesn't fade. I want to remember her smile, her laughter, the good times. But every time I think of her the same violent, twisted images flash on the screen of my mind so brightly, so harshly, that I can't see anything else. It's a blinding light that blots out everything – or it's a darkness so complete that all my senses are shut down.

I'm struggling for the words, I just can't tap into the memories I know are there. Lord, I can't cancel what has happened, the horror of it all. But help me, please help me, to unlock that store of pictures. The sounds, the everyday, loving things that filled up my senses when she was alive. When we lived and learned and shared life together. Please don't let me lose those memories, those times of joy.

Please God. Please!

*We try to mark the time, the place, the death of someone in significant and insignificant ways. At the time they all mean something and we should be allowed to begin to mark the importance and value of the person who has died, or been killed. This matters.*

## Flowers

Flowers,
ribbon tied to railings
or a tree.
A body dead?
A spirit flying free?
A sign of long-forgotten faith ...
revived?
A seeking after truth ...
or living grief?
Flowers wither ...
grief goes on ...
How long?
Oh God! How long?

*There has often been an assumption that children either don't grieve or that they should be shielded from grief. Frequently what is happening is that adults are covering the fact that they are worried about how they will grieve and, on top of everything else, what they will do with a grieving child. Only later, much later, they might be asked, 'Why didn't I go to Grandad's funeral?' The grief is there and it is real.*

*The first contact with death for some children may well be the death of a friend at school. The next two items just touch the edge of this grief.*

# Oh Jesus, can you hear my prayer

Oh Jesus, can you hear my prayer,
I feel so hurt inside;
I've never felt this way before,
I want to run and hide.

My friend has gone, I want to cry,
I don't know what to do;
they say that you will love me still,
I'm not sure if that's true.

O Jesus, will you stay by me
and help to dry my tears?
I want to play our games again
but all I feel are fears.

Oh Jesus will you be my friend?
I need a friend today;
someone to share the way I feel,
to hear the words I pray.

Tune:    Horsley
Metre:   CM

*This could be easily adapted to be sung by a group of children using 'our', 'we' and 'us'.*

# Dear God, it's so difficult

Dear God, it's so difficult to realize that we will never see our friend again.

When we remember that, it often makes us want to cry.

It hurts when we see the places where N used to be.

It's so sad that we can't talk and laugh together any more.

Some days and some things we do bring sad memories because N was always involved in them.

We pray for N's family and other friends and ask that you will be with them in their sorrow.

Jesus cried when his friend died, so we know that you understand our sadness.

Help us to help each other, by talking and listening and caring.

We need to share memories, as well as tears.

Loving God, look after us. Please.

*There are very few instances of suicide referred to in the Bible. To talk of suicide, for many generations, has been anathema. Suicide raises questions, generates guilt. It is a very aggressive act. Those who are left often struggle to answer the questions and shoulder the guilt. This reflection on Judas' suicide explores it from Peter's perspective.*

# Peter and the traitor

So! He's killed himself, has he? The traitor?
Couldn't live with his conscience.
I'm not surprised.
After all that time pretending to be a loyal follower, what does he do? He leads the authorities to Jesus in an isolated place, so there's no crowd to defend him and he even goes so far as to kiss Jesus to identify him.
Traitor! Betrayer! Hypocrite!
He deserves to die. And, if we'd got our hands on him ...!

But, listen to me. What am I saying? How can I condemn him? I betrayed Jesus too.
I said I didn't know him, instead of standing up for him. And Jesus knew that I'd done it; in fact, he even predicted that I would.

I still can't understand what made Judas do what he did.
There are all kinds of theories and rumours.
Some say he was a frustrated revolutionary who couldn't get Jesus to start a revolt. Some say he did it for the money. I don't think so, but there had been talk before then that he might be filching money from our common purse. Treasurers have been known to do that – often. Others think Judas was trying to push Jesus into making a stand and declaring a new kingdom. Maybe! But, if so, he got that very wrong, didn't he?

We'll never know now, will we? He's made sure of that. Dead men can't talk and he didn't confide in any of us about what he was thinking.

He was always a loner. The rest of us all came from Galilee; he was a Judean, so that didn't help. Soft southerners don't always take well to us blunt northerners and he was outnumbered, eleven to one. Different kind of people altogether, the Judeans. And he certainly liked to think he was important. When he was given charge of our money, you'd have thought he was in charge of the temple coffers, he made such a fuss about it. And he was always going on about how much good could be done for the poor, if people weren't so extravagant.
Hypocrite!
Then he goes behind our backs and betrays Jesus for money!

But it can't have been for the money. If he had the money, why kill himself?
And we've heard a rumour that he even went to try to give the money back!

No, there was more to it than that. I go for the revolution theory. If Judas was more of a hothead than we thought he was and he wanted to overthrow the Romans, maybe he was just trying to use Jesus to do that. Either he thought that Jesus was going to be in his way, because he was preaching non-violence and a changed attitude to life; or he thought he might force Jesus to act, if he was in real danger of execution.

They're the only ideas that make any sense at all. Judas had never shown any signs of hating Jesus, in fact he seemed very close to him. He even sat in the best place at that last supper we had together.
None of us noticed when he left the room, but if only we'd known ...

It's too late now. Jesus is dead and so is he.

And that's strange! Something must have gone very wrong with Judas' plans, if he decided to kill himself. If he'd been in league with the priests, surely he would have just gone over to their side and taken their protection.

Maybe he really did love Jesus.
Maybe he couldn't live with himself because he'd betrayed his friend. And killed him.

And I betrayed Jesus, too!
And I'll never know if he would have forgiven me.

Maybe Judas didn't believe anyone would ever forgive him. That's why he thought he'd be better off dead. What a desperate state to be in.

Should we have been able to predict it? To prevent it?

Too late now!

God knows! God alone knows the reasons.

*Suicide is aggressive and violent however it takes place. It hurts those who are left and is often constructed for that purpose. Faced with a suicide there are often more 'what ifs', more lingering guilt than with any other type of death. There are not always notes of explanation. When there are they often accuse the bereaved implicitly or explicitly.*

# This sugar-coated pill I hold

This sugar-coated pill I hold
within my shaking hand
was made to cure, to help, to heal,
how can I understand?

The jar is empty on the floor
and scattered all around,
the debris, evidence of life,
lies broken on the ground.
This room once echoed to her cry.
The baby that I bore
then grew beyond my scope to care,
yet I loved all the more.

And now, O God, what can I do
to fill this yawning void,
to answer questions, ease my guilt,
when love has been destroyed?

O hold me as I once held her
and never let me go.
O hold me till I cease to cry,
till no more tears can flow.
O hold me, love me, in the dark,
and through each lonely day
until the shadows start to shift
and I can find my way.

# Left ...

There are times when I am so angry with him.
How could he have done such a thing to me? Such a selfish thing!
He's now out of the picture. All his problems are solved.
He couldn't cope with life, so he ended it all.
Finished! Done! Let somebody else clear up the mess!
And that means me.
Didn't he recognize that the shock of finding him could have killed me?
Or was he so wrapped up in his own misery, that he didn't even consider that?
Oh, God. Why?
Why did he not talk about his despair?
Why didn't he trust me enough to try to explain?
How can I live with this guilt?
Should I have noticed something?
Will I ever forgive myself?
Or him?
Will I ever get over this?
God. If you're there and if you care, please listen and understand.
I need someone who can.

# I feel so guilty

I feel so guilty.

*But you could do nothing.*

I go through all the 'what ifs'.
No answers.
Just emptiness because I can't put the clock back, and if I did I probably wouldn't
    do things differently.
And if I did, would it have been different?
The truth is, I don't know.

*You love him. That's why you feel like this. That will never change.*
*Loving yourself is more difficult ... impossible perhaps.*

# Blessings

In the days when questions are insistent, but there are no answers,
God will listen patiently.
In the days when guilt is strong, but nothing can be changed,
God will understand and forgive.
In the days when anger rules, but striking out will not help,
God will wait to bring peace.
And in the days when there are no words, only tears,
God is still blessing you and watching over you.

Though your heart is broken, God will bring healing, when you are ready to receive it.
Though deep darkness fills your soul, God will not let the light go out completely.
Though the future holds no promise, God will not desert you.
Through the bleakest days, God will hold you, until you can begin to face life again.
God will bless you, for that is his promise.

# So where is God?

*disasters, war, terrorism, remembrance*

*When natural disasters occur, people wonder more than ever about God. They blame God. They question God's existence. They question the nature of God. They wonder that a so-called 'loving God' can allow such things to happen.*
*Psalmists wrote laments for a whole nation to share as well as for individuals to utter in desolation. We still need to enable such a response in today's world with all our scientific know-how and technological ability. This is because disasters still happen and questions still get asked even though we may never answer them satisfactorily. We still need to express our perplexity and grief.*

# As the dust has settled

As the dust has settled,
as your people die,
still we wait, and grieving,
ask the question 'Why?'

Here we find no answer
in this madding crowd;
here as faith is broken
dust becomes a shroud.

Dust to dust and ashes,
silently they lie.
All the world is silent,
yet earth seems to cry;

seems to cry in solace,
seems to offer grace,
finds a way to comfort:
God is in this place.

Tune:   Darwen
Metre:  6.5.6.5

# The people that we see

The people that we see
lie dying, dead or maimed.
No terrorist has caused this hell,
and no one can be blamed.

O God! what is your plan,
your narrative or art,
that needs the dying and the dead
to play this costly part?

We wait, we watch, we mourn.
In hopelessness we stand.
God, help your people find a source
of comfort in this land.

Tune:   Egham
Metre:  SM

# Tune: Egham

W. Turner (1651-1740)

1. The peo - ple that we see lie dy - ing, dead or maimed.

No terror - ist has cau - sed this hell, and no one can be blamed.

# Seeing death and desecration

Seeing death and desecration;
natural hazards, human fate,
is this part of God's creation?
Will the horror soon abate?
Through a feeling, more than reason,
just a glimpse of fleeting grace,
we will hold on, for a season,
to our damaged, limping faith.

Making sense of devastation,
human grief and mental pain,
moves us to the age-old question,
makes us plumb the depths again.
Who to blame and who to challenge?
Where is God amid the loss?
Where, when people have to scavenge,
is there meaning in a cross?

So we wait, belief in tatters;
struggle to retain our faith.
Every resolution shatters.
Certainties destroyed apace.
Yet we reach to sisters, brothers;
creeds, divisions turn to dust.
Now we feel at one with others;
enmity transformed to trust.

Tune:   Manor House
Metre:   8.7.8.7.D

*In recent times when disasters have struck or acts of terrorism have been perpetrated they have been utterly indiscriminate. People of many faiths and no faith have been equally maimed, killed or bereaved. Grief has sometimes had an international dimension. People with many different expressions of belief have found themselves side by side trying to cope with loss.*

# United in our common grief

United in our common grief, we pray to God by many names; we seek the power we need to find to hold us in this time of stress. Weeping, anger and fear are human reactions to tragedy and are shared by us all. Whatever our creed, race, or circumstances, we are affected by loss and need to find a way of expressing our shock and bewilderment.

We pray for understanding and for the strength and courage to cope with what has happened. As we share with one another, help us to find comfort in our companionship and active love through our common concern. We pray for all those who have suffered and all who have died. We ask for healing and hope to restore shattered lives and for courage and determination to begin to build for the future.

Hold us through our grief.
Understand our anger and our questions.
Unite us in our concern and action and reassure us that this tragedy can be overcome.
God of many names and faces, bless us at this time, and hold us through all that lies ahead.

# The undercurrent breaks our grip

The undercurrent breaks our grip
on sand that shifts and sways;
this grief has come to taunt our faith:
is this a cause for praise?

Disasters shake and tear the world
as people kneel in prayer.
In random tragedy and pain
we chant 'Our God is there'.

If God is there, what sort of God
would watch these people die,
would see young babies swept away
and still ignore their cry?

We haven't found the answer yet
to cosmic suffering:
we cry to God, our trust remains
although faith cannot sing.

Tune:    St Columba
Metre:   CM

*Worldwide communications bring us face to face with the suffering of others across the globe almost instantaneously. We either turn away or empathize. There seems to be no middle way.*

# In every face we see the pain

In every face we see the pain
of grief and human loss;
the hell we cannot understand,
we cannot count the cost.
In each disaster we recount
earth's shifting, changing ways.
Creation brings its agony,
a challenge to our praise.

And was God midwife at the birth
confounding our belief?
Or is our God outside the frame,
removed from human grief?
For ages we have tried and failed
to understand this flaw,
that God should let such evil rise,
while mixing love and awe.

If God is here, where bodies break,
where life seems so much dross,
where is the mercy, grace and love
the gift of crib and cross?
We plead for love, we long for grace,
to help us, where they fell,
to grasp the reason for this pain,
this cavalcade of hell.

Then give us strength to rise again,
enlivened by your hope,
and for the present show your love
and give us grace to cope.
God come and join your people in
the centre of their loss.
If you are real then show yourself
upon this present cross.

Tune:    Kingsfold
Metre:   DCM

# Creator God

Creator God, whose world is one family, help us to recognize our common humanity.

For wherever they are, victims of terrorism cry out in bitter anguish; bombs and shells kill soldiers and civilians alike; homes and businesses are shattered and broken; rescuers search rubble for faint signs of life; bereaved  children weep bewildered tears; family units are torn apart by destruction; refugees lose their dignity and sense of identity; peace is shattered.

Keep us alert to the tears and fears that are our common experience. Open our hands and hearts in sympathy and understanding. Show us how to express our care in practical ways. Please, Lord.

God of peace, whose world is torn apart by evil, greed, power and cruelty, help us to be active in our work for peace.

For all over your world power corrupts and greed distorts values; evil has no conscience; terrorists justify actions by perverted logic; prejudice feeds fear and fear promotes violence; weapons of mass destruction are dangerously active; ignorance promotes hostility, danger is at hand.

Help us to find the truth behind the propaganda.
Give us an insight into the part we play ourselves and a will to be changed when we work against your loving purpose.
Teach us to promote peaceful ways and positive thoughts. Give us the courage to tackle prejudice where we find it. Show us how to face up to evil and defeat it.
In your name, Lord and for your sake.

*Like the Psalmists we can, and perhaps we ought to, lament.*

# We once acclaimed your name as 'Love'

We once acclaimed your name as 'Love'.
Were we so very wrong?
We watch, and helplessly we cry:
'How long, O God, how long'?

How long, O God, shall we endure
through earthquake, wind and wave?
We witness, yet again, the scenes
which make our faith less brave.

Our hist'ry says you brought release,
to those enslaved by hate;
and now in hope, we form our prayer,
that suff'ring might abate.

You said that you would offer hope
and tend the damaged reed,
that you would fan the flame of love,
and nurture hidden seed.

Come soon and bring relief to those
who suffer human pain,
come soon and hear our plea, O God,
let no one cry in vain.

Tune:   Crimond
Metre:   CM

# Whatever way we name our God

Whatever way we name our God,
if by a name at all,
within this common shroud of grief
we hear each other call.

We share a human bond of pain,
we hold with human care,
while shattered lives command our love
and fear is everywhere.

Our tears transcend each word and creed,
the things we see and hear
cut to the very core of life,
the centre of our fear.

So hand in hand and side by side
we'll face the fact of death,
together we will seek new hope
as long as we have breath.

Tune:   Wiltshire
Metre:   CM

*We need to make sense of war and terrorism, to find ways of living as Christians in the midst of a violent world. We should be open to questioning, even if that questioning might give expression to doubt. If we are not honest in this way, we merely add to the problems we are facing and our faith is literally incredible to those around us.*

*It is important to make sense of our faith in the light of our experience.*

# God would not will what we have seen

God would not will what we have seen,
the terror, war and death;
for God is love, the source of life,
the essence of our breath.

God would not break the damaged reed,
the smouldering wick is fanned;
yet human power, our want and greed
can counter what God planned.

Our will is free, our way we choose,
to act for good or ill,
to offer love, to calm or heal,
to damage or to kill.

God give us courage in the face
of carnage that we see,
to work for life, to live for love,
to set your people free.

Tune: Horsley
Metre: CM

# Insidious clouds – the terror spreads

Insidious clouds – the terror spreads
as few are peaceful in their beds,
while cries are silenced by the roar
of fire as flames consume and soar.

And where is God when hatred burns?
Remote and safe beyond concerns?

*A stable birth once gave the lie,
as did a mother's tear and sigh;*

*For, as she stood beneath a cross
and shared forsakenness and loss;
so now God dies a thousand deaths
and mothers gasp a thousand breaths.*

The flames consume and lick and soar,
above the war planes dive and roar,

*and in another cradle bed
an orphaned child lays down her head.*

You ask where is your God tonight?
So very near, not out of sight.

*Too weak to help and needing love,
she reaches to you, looks above.*

# All-knowing God

All-knowing God, you understand the way we struggle with life and death. So we bring our prayers to you, and lay our problems at your feet.

We pray for those who are wrestling with the issues of war and peace. These matters are never clear-cut and violent reactions are never guaranteed to bring peace, yet evil must be defeated – and there is so much evil in the world. Be with all those who are trying to bring peace into situations of conflict. We pray for politicians and all those with influence and power. Open their minds to constructive ways of peacemaking and conflict resolution. Bless all innocent victims of war, who have no place to go to escape and no homes when it all ends. Bless those in the armed forces whose job it is to fight when they are told – and especially bless those who are urged to fight for a cause they don't understand, by people who have their own evil motives. Father, forgive them, for they do not know what they are doing.

*God can cope with our cries for help.*

# Homes that once held joy and laughter

Homes that once held joy and laughter,
faces we no longer see,
all are smeared by this disaster,
torn by common tragedy.
Death has come, and faith is broken,
love has little courage left,
God we cry in desolation,
hold us as we stand bereft.

As we stand by one another,
fractured by this common grief,
with your grace and love enfold us,
hold us, heal our disbelief;
hold us crippled by this sorrow,
hold us till the crying clears,
hold us through each frail tomorrow,
through this cavalcade of fears.

Here amid this desecration,
mid the wreckage of our lives,
where despair hangs like a shadow,
hardly any hope survives.
All our wealth, our worldly riches,
cannot stem this sense of pain;
so, confronted by this horror,
God, give grace to build again.

Tune:   Abbot's Leigh
Metre:  8.7.8.7.D

# What do we do? How can we cope

What do we do? How can we cope
with random violence such as this?
We feel again the pain of death,
receive again betrayal's kiss.

Where is the love that once we knew,
protection that we thought was ours,
as God-forsaken now we stand
where lives are torn and courage cowers.

Come to our aid. O hear our cry,
as, faced with carnage death and fear,
we struggle to contain our hate
and need to know your love is near.

Tune:   Arizona
Metre:  LM

# Tune: Arizona

R.H. Eaushaw (1856-1929)

1. What do we do? How can we cope with ran - dom vi - o - lence such as this? We feel a - gain the pain of death, re - ceive a - gain be - tray - al's kiss.

*Christian theology leads us to believe that when we suffer God suffers with us. When life is damaged God shares the pain. That is part of the message of the incarnation, the coming of God into the world in the person of Jesus. The other side of the coin is the Christian belief that when we reach out, as Jesus might have done, we become as Jesus to the person. We can be real and effective channels of God's comfort, healing and love.*

# Each groan of pain from tortured lips

Each groan of pain from tortured lips,
each tear that falls from anguished eyes,
the slightest murmur of a sigh,
as yet another victim dies,
are nails into the hands of Christ
counting against the tyrant's lies.

Each agony of starving death,
each haunted look of gaunt despair;
the scrabbling hands that search the dirt
although the earth is cracked and bare,
are echoes in the mind of Christ
of his last agonizing prayer.

Each home destroyed by missile blast,
each terror of a war-torn land,
the crying of a frightened child
alone without a loving hand,
are spears pierced in the side of Christ
and pain which he can understand.

Each empty mind which sees no pain,
each ignorance of crying need,
the pleas of those who go unheard
while others wallow in their greed,
are thorns upon the brow of Christ
and open wounds that tear and bleed.

Each healing touch relieving pain,
each voice which speaks aloud for peace,
the giving hearts and willing hands
working so poverty may cease
are living out the words of Christ,
striving to give his love release.

Tunes:   Bannerman or Abingdon
Metre:   8.8.8.8.8.8.

# Tune: Bannerman

Paul Bateman (1954- )

Each groan of pain from tor-tured lips, each tear that falls from an - guished eyes, the slight-est mur - mur of a sigh, as yet a - no-ther vic - tim dies, are nails in - to the hands of Christ count-ing a - gainst the ty - rant's lies. Each a-gon

*In recent years we have witnessed public outpourings of grief which have been quite spontaneous. The death of Princess Diana may have marked the start of this. To many people these actions have been inexplicable. They have been dismissed as signs of hysteria and self-gratification. Sometimes they have been just that. At other times there seems to have been a true expression of grief. Maybe such public events allow us to tap into grief that we have buried, allowing us to grieve.*

# The flower carpet grows

The flower carpet grows and keeps on growing,
row upon row of wrappings, ribbons, roses,
flowers rotting, messages erased by tears and rain.
Candles make shrines, pinpoints of light
overhung by shadowed faces keeping vigil.
Complete strangers embrace and weep together
and pain is etched on faces, young and old.
This public show of grief seems strange, unnatural,
yet grief is raw and, in most cases, real.
Is it for this death that they cry?
Or is it that tragedy
touches the grief we hide within,
emotion held in check?

So, seeing others weep, we weep with them.

We watch the flower carpet grow
and know that we may lay our flowers
at the shrine of memory
and weep the tears that need release.

*A soldier from the First World War told the story of holding the hand of his dying friend:*

# No armistice

No armistice
and every day a memory,
not remembrance.
Survival's guilt hangs heavy
like a shroud.
The frightened eyes,
the failing breath,
the flailing limbs,
I will never forget.
Never forget.
Decades pass,
yet nothing fades,
vivid as yesterday
the violence,
the carnage,
flamed on the retina
of my mind.
I hold his hand,
hear his voice,
he slips away,
is,
yet is no more,
And
at the going down of the sun
and in every blazing,
blinding moment
I will remember him.
God where is your victory?
Death, I feel your sting.
Christ!
hold me.

*Even our prayer can move us to action.*

# Sometimes we feel such utter loss

Sometimes we feel such utter loss
confronted by the world's despair,
the scenes of human agony,
of lives destroyed, of absent care.

When Jesus touched a broken man,
despised because of leprosy,
he felt his hurt and shared his pain,
and challenged our hypocrisy.

Yet still we watch and wring our hands,
avoid responsibility,
but if we felt another's pain,
our lives would act in sympathy.

So while we share this agony
half understanding pained despair,
O God give loving empathy,
at least enable active prayer.

Tune:   Martham
Metre:  LM

*Remembrance of those who have died is imperative, particularly if those people died in war. Sometimes such death came to people who were committed to the cause for which they were fighting. Sometimes they had been manipulated by those with more power and put into situations that they would not have chosen, yet could not avoid. For some their death was unmarked and there is no body, no grave. Some were deemed cowards for deserting when they simply could take no more. All are remembered by those who love them. All are God's and their parents' children.*

# By a monument of marble

By a monument of marble,
or by simple wooden cross,
here we gather to remember
sacrifice and tragic loss.
Blood-red poppy petals flutter,
shadows of a war long past:
all the conflict, all the carnage
sanitized by time at last.

Solemn silence now surrounds us
as we stand in memory.
Why should evil lead to conflict?
This eternal mystery
troubles hearts and stirs the conscience,
urges us to think again;
face the curse of confrontation,
yet reduce this searing pain.

For the sound of war still thunders
through our planet, on this day.
Every hour new victims suffer,
even as we meet to pray.
God, beyond our understanding,
peace seems far beyond our reach;
move us on to new solutions
through that active love you teach.

Tune:   Lux Eoi
Metre:  8 7 8 7 D

# Tune: Lux Eoi

A. Sullivan (1842–1900)

1. By a mon-u-ment of mar-ble, or by sim-ple wood-en cross,

here we ga-ther to re-mem-ber sac-ri-fice and tra-gic loss.

Blood-red pop-py pe-tals flut-ter, shad-ows of a war long past:

all the con-flict, all the carn-age san-i-tized by time at last.

# Blessings

When the world around is shattered and torn,
God holds us through shock and bewilderment.
When another disaster appears to be inexplicable,
God listens to our rage and hears our questions.
When the death toll is horrendous and injuries change lives for ever,
God weeps and wonders with us.
When the future must be faced, as practicalities of living begin to surface,
God waits to guide us into this new unknown.
God cares – even when it seems that there is no God at all.


God will be with you in the desolation of your days.
God will be with you in the darkest of your nights.
God will be with you in hopelessness and despair.
God will be with you in fear and anger.
God will be with you when all reason has gone.
God will be with you to love and to cherish you
until you are ready to face life again.
God will be with you.

# New beginnings

*facing the present and
meeting the future*

*When someone dies life never returns to normal, if by that we mean life as it was with that person. They are dead and no matter how strong our faith, they are no longer physically there. Somehow we have to adjust. Somehow we need to go forward, not denying the person's existence or value to us, but taking that into account as we frame a new way of living. Perhaps we will try to keep their memory alive with a memorial or by things that we do. But we cannot escape the cold, sober fact that they are dead. So we make a new beginning.*

# Endings

'This is the end,'
said Moses
as he saw the Red Sea cross his path,
a barrier to freedom.
And yet today
the Jews still celebrate their crossing
as a turning point
within their history.

'This is the end,'
said Elijah
hiding in his mountain cave,
cowering from danger.
And yet, from there,
through howling wind and storming rain
he saw God's power
within the stillness.

'This is the end,'
said Mary
bent with sorrow at the cross's foot
where hung her son.
And yet she heard
'Take care of her', and felt his love
surround her even then
within the arms of John.

'This is the end,'
said Jesus
as his tortured body gave itself to death
and darkness fell.
And yet he knew
this end was but a new beginning.
No power of Rome or priest could keep the
        love of God
within a tomb.

'This is the end,'
we say
when life is torn apart
by tragic loss.
And yet, beyond our grief,
the pain-filled eyes of a Father,
whose Son faced death too soon,
are weeping with us.

*Coming to terms with the fact of death is not easy. We will want to deny it. We are likely to be angry, to bargain our way out of grief. But ultimately we have to face the fact of death if we are ever to move on, to live instead of simply existing.*

# This fact I have to face today

This fact I have to face today,
this fact that death would not delay;
yet faith proclaims a brighter day
Alleluia!

I own the ones I love can die,
I own a truth and not a lie;
and yet with God this song they cry:
Alleluia!

Though years have passed, I still feel pain,
and memories will still remain,
but now I'm free to praise again
Alleluia!

Tune: Vulpius
Metre: 8.8.8.8. Alleluia

# It had hung over me like a heavy, dark pall

It had hung over me like a heavy, dark pall. Sometimes the grief would swirl, choking, disabling me so my legs felt like lead; my breathing laboured, heavy, breathless. There seemed no end to this. Any respite was temporary, the cloud descending again without warning, as soon as it had fully lifted. Months lengthened into years. You become accustomed to the darkness, feeling your way without purpose or motivation.

Then almost as sudden as death, the pain, the anger, swept softly away like mist dispersed by a morning breeze ... and I can't explain that. There seems to be nothing rational to it. But I know it happened. All the words that had seemed empty, mere platitudes, began to make sense again. I could sing of resurrection and I meant it. This was not some great conversion, yet it was, I suppose. It was certainly the beginning of something different, the stirrings of renewed faith. Resurrection, yes resurrection; I had started to live again. And I thank God for that.

# As dawn is breaking in the sky

*For some the image of a new day, the changing of the seasons, can be helpful metaphors to remind us of God's continuing presence with us in spite of death.*

As dawn is breaking in the sky
and darkness creeps away,
the world awakes to light and life
and thankful Christians pray,
for God renews our trust again
as night turns into day.

# I saw the sun rise again this morning

As scars we leave upon the land
are changed again to green,
when nature turns the pages back
with seeds that slept unseen;
then God renews the earth again
and recreates the scene.

I saw the sun rise again this morning,
as I have done so often in these past months,
after yet another sleepless night.
But this morning I watched the faintest light
creep slowly into the darkness.
I noticed how the rooftops started to
    take shape.
I was aware of how the colour crept back in
to change the picture and to bring it back
    to life.
And, as the sky took on the blaze of pink,
orange, gold, and then the blinding light
of morning sun,
I recognized that I was seeing,
feeling, experiencing
the birth of a new day –
and it held meaning.

As pain and sorrow, hurt and grief
are touched by Christian care,
which in compassion reaches out
to answer anguished prayer;
then God renews our hope again
by showing he is there.

So let us join to praise the God
who meets our daily needs
and dedicate ourselves again
to Christian words and deeds,
as we renew the vows we made
to follow where he leads.

Tune:    Sheltered Dale
Metre:   8.6.8.6.8.6

Dear God, is this a significant moment?
Are you trying to say something to me?
My life has been shrouded in darkness.
Is it now time to let the light creep in?

God of dawn, hold me safely
as I begin to step out into the light
for I must now begin to live again.

*Sometimes it will be much later before we realize that even in our deepest grief God was there and never let us go.*

# My God, how wonderful your love

My God, how wonderful your love,
your scope of care and grace,
you saw the depth of my distress
before I glimpsed your face.

You reached to heal my deepest hurt,
to comfort and restore,
before I fully understood
all you had done before.

You'd shared my sadness, horror, loss,
my hopelessness and pain,
you waited with me in my grief:
I learned to live again.

You walked beside me all my way,
you joined my dance of joy,
you opened up a way to hope
that nothing could destroy.

Tune:    Westminster (Turle)
Metre:   CM

*Sometimes we have to wait a long time for comfort to come, to feel that we matter to anyone, let alone to God. Then we are surprised when out of the blue we have a moment of relief. It may be ever so brief. But then it happens again and we begin to realize that we have intrinsic value which has not and cannot be diminished by the loss of the one we have loved so completely. While we are waiting, if others sense our need, we will continue to be held in human love.*

# Thanks be to God for the gifts that are hidden

Thanks be to God for the gifts that are hidden,
waiting the spirit to stir them again,
signs of the grace that can lighten our burden,
gifts that are shrouded, yet always remain.

Thanks be to God for the ones who would
        hold us,
even when daylight is darker than night.
Thanks be to God for the love that enfolds us,
bringing us back from our grief to the light.

Thanks be to God for the ones who remind us
faith is still there, though the clouds hide
        our view;
people God offers when spiritual blindness
needs love to heal, to restore and renew.

Tune:    Stewardship
Metre:   11.10.11.10

*Gradually faith returns, though it will probably be so radically different that those who know us may not even recognize it as faith. Then we will be able to go forward into the future with hope.*

# With daring we enter the future that beckons

With daring we enter the future that beckons,
our feelings in tension – excitement and fear.
Wherever we're walking we know God walks
    with us,
before and behind, God's protection is near.

Alone in the desert God's people felt empty,
the land that was promised of honey and milk
seemed distant, reality made hope distorted,
clothed them with despairing, more sackcloth
    than silk.

And sometimes the way that we find in the
    present
has troubles and heartaches enough of its
    own;
but still God walks with us through valleys of
    darkness,
encompassed with loving, we're never alone.

So welcome the future and enter it boldly,
look back, God was with you wherever you
    trod.
This God is your lover through life and
    forever,
take hold of the certainty: this is your God.

Tune:    Helsington or Was lebet, was schwebet
Metre:   12.11.12.11

# I didn't go to her grave today

I didn't go to her grave today ...

... and for the first time, I didn't feel guilty
    about that.
So much of my grief is wrapped up in myself,
almost as if I'm blaming her for leaving me.
Or, am I blaming God that she is gone?

But today, I didn't go to see her grave.
She is not there,
only her body – the shell of what she was –
still is, to me.
The shell I can let go in time.
The essence of her is around me here.
Is this what they call resurrection?

I didn't go to see her grave today,
but I thanked God
that I had shared my life with her.

# God marks no ending, only new beginnings

God marks no ending, only new beginnings,
until the consummation of our lives;
God keeps no count of losses, nor of winnings:
we move through grace, the holy spirit thrives.

So as we go beyond this time, this setting,
rememb'ring all the laughter and the tears;
we go with God in faith, so not regretting
the moments shared, the hopes, the dreams, the fears.

Though parted for a while, we travel onward,
not knowing what the future has in store.
This phase will close, the spirit draws us forward,
we've tasted love, but God has promised more!

Tune:    Lord for the years
Metre:   11.10.11.10

*Slowly we discover that God's love is constant, unwavering, whatever life may have thrown at us, whatever grief we may have had to bear.*

# Bright morning maker

Bright morning maker, as your sun breaks through,
dawn's early light reflects in morning dew.
So thankful people sing their praise to you:
Alleluia

Daylight creator, through the busy day,
sun, chasing shadows, drives the clouds away
and in the rush of life we pause to say:
Alleluia

Lifetime companion, in the evening light,
sunset throws colours at the approaching night
and weary hearts are lifted by the sight:
Alleluia

Night-time's safe keeper, when we take our rest,
lift darkening fears from those who are distressed.
Grant us your peace and may our sleep be blessed:
Alleluia

Tune:   Constancy (David McCarthy) or Sine Nomine
Metre:  10 10 10 4

# Tune: Constancy

David McCarthy (1931- )

1. Bright morn - ing ma - ker, as your sun breaks through,____ dawn's ear - ly light re - flects in mor - ning dew.____ So thank - ful peo - ple sing their praise to you: Al - le - lu – ia, al - le - !u – ia.

*When we grieve any moments of happiness can make us feel very guilty. Gradually we will cope with joy again. That may come as a bit of a surprise. God is there, has never gone away, is woven into the very fabric of our lives.*

# Surprised by joy that sets our spirits singing

Surprised by joy that sets our spirits singing
as, by this grace, we face a new beginning.
We sense God's presence woven through our story,
the sky and all the world is flamed with glory;
and all the earth is filled with praise,
sing alleluia all our days!

Amazed by love that counters expectation,
that finds us when we feel beyond redemption,
that reaches into hell to keep and hold us,
that uses human arms to warm, enfold us;
and all the earth is filled with praise,
sing alleluia all our days!

Still stunned by God, by providence and caring,
that shares in every trouble we are bearing.
Christ looks through eyes enlivened with compassion
to show such love that only God could fashion.
So all the earth is filled with praise!
Sing alleluia all our days!

Tune:    Surprised by joy (June Baker)
Metre:   11.11.11.11.8.8

# Tune: Surprised by joy

June Baker (1936- )

Sur - prised by joy that sets our spi-rits sing-ing_____ as,

by this grace, we face a new be-gin-ning. We sense God's pres - ence wov - en thro' our

sto - ry, the sky and all the world is flamed with glo - ry; and all the

earth is filled with praise,_____ sing all - e - lu - ia all our days!

119

# God the weaver, making patterns

God the weaver, making patterns,
spinning threads throughout our days –
joy and sadness interwoven,
strands of sorrow, strands of praise.
Help us to discern your weaving
in the multi-coloured maze.

Teach us, Lord, to trust your guidance
when the pattern is not clear,
and to feel your strength and comfort
when life's fabric's torn by fear.
Help us sense that in the dark times
lightening love is always near.

When we see the pattern changing
and a new direction starts,
let us know your love unbroken
winds through life in all its parts
by the threads of love and friendship
closely woven in our hearts.

Though we never see the picture
with your sense of space and time,
help us, Lord, to take our places
in our faith's continuing line,
as all lives are interwoven
in your final grand design.

Tune:    Perspective (David McCarthy)
Metre:   8.7.8.7.8.7.

# Tune: Perspective

David McCarthy (1931- )

God the wea ver, mak ing pat terns, spin ning threads through out our days – joy and sad ness in ter wov en, strands of sor row, strands of praise. Help us to dis cern your weav ing in the mul ti co loured maze.

*As God has been with you, even when that has seemed the furthest from the truth, we pray that you will be sure that God continues with you into all the future has to bring.*

# Blessings

God be with you and to bless you.
God use other arms to hold you.
God will carefully enfold you.
God will grant you peaceful sleeping.
God will greet you when awaking.


God go with you, wherever you go.
Each challenge he will meet with you.
In change he will adapt with you.
Through fear, he will strengthen you.
Through doubt, he will sustain you.
In hope he will encourage you.
In achievement he will rejoice with you.
At each turning of life he will be waiting for you.
Into his care we give you.

# Snowdrops

Imagine green leaves turning to brown in autumn beauty.
Under foot leaves darken, mulch down, crumble.
Snow settles, covering dull, dark earth with a white blanket,
beautiful, but cold and smothering.

Through that cold,
out of the crusted, hardened earth, a fine green spear pushes toward hidden light.
Bright, pristine, fragile, small, the first snowdrop is born.
You see it and know that there is hope, that beauty is not lost,
that love and joy and life, though dormant, are not dead.
Always remember to look for the snowdrops,
to nurture them, gather them, hold them, protect them.
They hold our dreams,
make them real, assure us that love does not falter or end.
Hold fast to the most precious gift:
remember, God loves you.

God will hold you through the cold times, the dark times, those times like death.
God will nurture and care for you.
God will fold and enfold you in love.
God will warm you and find the joy, dormant in your heart.
You will share that love, celebrate it
and rest in it always.

The items marked S&B are © Stainer & Bell Ltd, P.O. Box 110, Victoria House, 23 Gruneisen Road, London N3 1DZ and those marked CJM Music Ltd are © CJM Music Ltd, Don Bosco House, Country Road, Coleshill B46 3EA.

# Thematic index